What in the World Am I Doing Here?

The Christian Faith and Personal Mission

Terry Swan

What In The World Am I Doing Here?

The Christian Faith And Personal Mission

PUBLISHING

Belleville, Ontario, Canada

What in the World Am I Doing Here?

Copyright © 2003, Terry Swan

Scriptures marked NIV are from *The Holy Bible, New International Version.* Copyright © 1973, 1978, 1984 International Bible Society. Used by permission of Zondervan Publishing House. All rights reserved. Scriptures marked KJV are from *The Holy Bible, King James Version.* Copyright © 1977, 1984, Thomas Nelson Inc., Publishers. Scripture quotations marked NKJV are taken from the *New King James Version.* Copyright © 1979, 1980, 1982. Thomas Nelson Inc., Publishers. Scripture quotations not marked otherwise are the author's paraphrase.

First Printing: July 2003	**Second Printing**: August 2005
Third Printing July 2009	**Fourth Printing** July 2010
Fifth Printing August 2011	**Sixth Printing** July 2013
Seventh Printing August 2014	**Eighth Printing** September 2016

National Library of Canada Cataloguing in Publication
Swan, Terry, 1953-
   What in the world am I doing here? / Terry Swan.
Includes bibliographical references.
ISBN 978-1-55306-651-0.--ISBN 1-55306-653-7 (LSI ed.)   1.
Christian life. I. Title.

BV4501.3.S82 2003   248.4   C2003-903854-8

E-book ISBN: 978-1-55452-992-6
(E-book available from the Kindle Store, KOBO and the iBookstore)

Essence Publishing is a Christian Book Publisher dedicated to furthering the work of Christ through the written word. For more information, contact:

20 Hanna Court, Belleville, Ontario, Canada K8P 5J2
Phone: 1-800-238-6376 • Fax: (613) 962-3055
E-mail: info@essence-publishing.com
Web site: www.essence-publishing.com

Table of Contents

Think of me as a fellow-patient in the same hospital who, having been admitted a little earlier, could give some advice.

—C.S. LEWIS

Asking the right questions takes as much skill as giving the right answer.

—ROBERT HALF

Call to me and I will answer you and tell you great and unsearchable things you do not know.

—JEREMIAH 33:3, NKJV

Millions long for immortality who don't know what to do with themselves on a rainy Sunday afternoon.

—SUSAN ERTZ

We must be willing to get rid of the life we've planned, so as to have the life that is waiting for us.

—JOSEPH CAMPBELL

But yield who will to their separation,
My object in living is to unite
My avocation and my vocation
As my two eyes make one in sight.
Only where love and need are one,
And the work is play for mortal stakes,
Is the deed ever really done
For Heaven and the future's sakes.

—ROBERT FROST
From "Two Tramps in Mud Time."

What in the World Am I Doing Here?

I'm an early riser. Always have been. No matter what time I go to bed, I seem to wake up around 5:30 a.m. My wife calls me the human alarm clock. Benjamin Franklin said that early to bed, early to rise, makes a man healthy, wealthy and wise. I am healthy anyway, so I guess one out of three isn't bad!

Early morning is a special time to me. It's quiet. No one is demanding my attention. The phone is not ringing. I organize my day, have my devotional time, get centered, do my writing and exercise. I do a lot of thinking in the early morning hours when I'm at my peak.

Not long ago, I stepped outside early in the morning to pick up the newspaper. I paused to look up into what was an absolutely crisp and clear sky. Stars were everywhere. It was majestic. Simply awesome.

As I stood there, the words of my earlier devotional reading from Scripture came into my head:

> When I consider your handiwork, the work of your fin-
> gers, the moon and the stars which you have set in place,
> what is man that you are mindful of him, the son of man

that you care for him? You made him a little lower than heavenly beings and crowned him with glory and honor.[1]

In writing this psalm, King David was asking a deeply existential question that we must all ask of ourselves: What in the world am I doing here? Small me, living in the midst of this big world.

David believed, and we affirm, that our lives only produce eternal meaning in relationship to God and God's will. So... why did God pick you? How does God care for you? And, in your world, your orbit of influence, how do you understand your personal, unique mission on earth? What in the world *are* you doing here?

If you thought of your life as a movie, what would the various scenes look like? On the average, a motion picture consists of 132 scenes. A producer carefully chooses the scenes that will best illustrate the storyline. This is true from beginning to end. How would you anticipate the plot all the way through to the ending for the movie entitled *Your Life*?

Let's think together about the significant question of your existence—the "*I*" part of *what in the world am I doing here*? The Bible clearly states that God chose you—you didn't choose God. God foreordained you from the beginning of time.[2]

It may be difficult to grasp how special this makes you in God's sight. For you will only know who you are when you know *whose* you are. You have value and worth in just being God's chosen one.

Over the past three decades in Western civilization, we have rather swiftly moved towards becoming what philosophers would call a utilitarian society. That is, we do not value people for just being human beings. We value them for what they can contribute to society. This is their utility, their usefulness, and it is a very dangerous and unbiblical view of human beings.

When we value people for what they can contribute, then two groups at opposite ends of the age spectrum become extremely at risk. Which two age groups in the early twenty-first century are most impacted by a utilitarian world view? The elderly… and the unborn.

For the very elderly, we see euthanasia slowly creeping into acceptance in our culture. We are only a couple short steps from ending Great-Grandma's life because she has nothing tangible to contribute to a secular society anymore.

For the unborn, we know of nearly forty million abortions since the 1973 Roe vs. Wade decision. When I speak to my college classes, I tell them that if they were born since 1973, they should get on their knees and thank God for their getting out of the womb alive, because one in every four classmates didn't make it that far. Twenty five percent never got a chance.

Some call the current group of young adults "the Holocaust generation." Forty million human beings. Not fetuses. Not tissue. Not a choice. For Scripture clearly says you were known and formed in the womb. You were not a potential human being, but a human being with potential.

So you, dear reader, are a very fortunate person. It's such a blessing just to be alive. And, like David, you may ask "Why me?" or maybe, "Is it just little me in the huge universe?"

The answer is, just little you and God. That's a powerful team. It's reminiscent of the elephant and mouse that crossed a bridge together. The bridge creaked and groaned as they went over it. On the other side, the mouse turned to the elephant and exclaimed, "Boy! We sure shook that bridge, didn't we?"

When it's you and God, you can shake the world. Kyle Macy was a former teammate of basketball's great Michael Jordan on the Chicago Bulls. He was the other guard in the backcourt the night Jordan scored 63 points against the Boston Celtics. Or, the way Macy put it, "It was the night Michael Jordan and I combined for 70 points against the Celtics." Just you and a big God can do wondrous things.

This leads us to the *doing* portion of the question—what in the world am I *doing* here? Occasionally you have moments of clarity in your life when you see things as they really are. I had one of those moments in early adulthood when I asked myself this question regarding what I was doing. I was nineteen years old, home on leave from the Army. I had changed in my year away. I'd matured. I'd renewed my faith commitment in many of my personal practices; I was quite a different person.

One night, I went to a dance hall in a nearby city for a reunion with several of my old high-school buddies. We spent a couple hours there, sitting around, and then the rock band took a break. A popular song came over the jukebox. It was a song with coarse lyrics and everybody joined in, singing along. I remember looking around the room. My buddies were getting brain-dead drunk. People were staggering by. The hall was filled with the crude lyrics of the song. I thought to myself, "What in the world am I doing here?" I excused myself, got up from the table, left and never returned.

The psalmist wrote, "I have considered my ways and have turned my steps to your statutes."[3] In that moment of clarity I realized that I was now on a different path. I was different. I was chosen. I'd made a decision to live my life with higher principles. It impacted all I said and did. I was now looking back at my former life with its fading practices and habits. That was over half my life ago, and seems to have been a person I never was; yet, the deep question of purpose and productivity—the "*doing*" of my life—has only expanded. My new life was to be lived before God. The Psalmist wrote, "All my ways are before thee."[4] Everything I did was seen by an omniscient, omnipresent, loving God.

It's like your life's movie is on a big-screen television before God. You can turn and look up into the camera right now, to the God before whom the secrets of all hearts are disclosed. The whole company of heaven watches. God sees what we are doing and wants to redeem the hours and days for nobler purposes.

God wants to use you. That's why you're alive. Whether you're eighteen or eighty, you must ask God, "What am I doing here?"

The final part of the question has to do with what am I doing *here*? Right here. The place you are now. Are you blooming where you are planted?

Early in young adulthood, I occasionally suffered from what could be called "destination disease." This mindset is where you're always looking to some other place, another job, a different partner; something you believe will bring you deep satisfaction. Always searching for "greener grass." In fact, before we can be happy anywhere else, we have to be content where we are now. This is the only moment in time that is yours—right now. So, learn to live in this moment. Be fully into your sphere of influence, your part of the universe.

Ann Keimel once wrote that she was out to change her world. That's the essence of the idea. Start small. Look around and see where you're needed.

George Washington Carver once prayed, "O, Lord, the world is just so big. What can I do? I'm so small in this needy world." Carver reported that God spoke to him and said, "George, how about a peanut? Take a little peanut and do something with it."

So, George Washington Carver took a peanut and, through experimentation, created over three hundred uses for it. With his research, he helped rebuild the economy of the South.

Start small, change your world. That's why you've been placed where you are.

We are not just human beings having a temporal spiritual experience. We are spiritual beings having a temporal human experience.

—TEILHARD DE CHARDIN

"He never knew who he was"

—BIFF, SPEAKING ABOUT HIS FATHER
in Arthur Miller's *Death of a Salesman*

All the days ordained for me were written in your book before one of them came to be.

—PSALM 139:16, NIV

We are human beings, not human doings.

—ANONYMOUS

We know what we are, but we know not what we may become.

—OPHELIA IN SHAKESPEARE'S HAMLET

I wish I were what I was when I was trying to become what I am now.

—BATHROOM GRAFFITI

*I'm a man and a man's a mixture right down from his very birth.
For part of him comes from heaven and part of him comes from earth.*

—STUDDERT KENNEDY

Who Am I?

"What I am to be, I am now becoming"

You are a complex person. To try and grasp the essence of who you are is an intimidating task.

Novelist William Faulkner once attempted to capture the human experience by reducing it to a single sentence in literature. He knew this was impossible, but he tried anyway. Thus, in his well-known 1942 story, "The Bear," Faulkner created an 1800-word sentence!

Language has its limitations, for we are intricate and eternal creatures. We cannot be captured in a single sentence or even in a book. Our earthly lives are only the cover page of the story.

And covers can conceal. Much like the concealing outer packaging for the grocery items you purchase, our present lives may mask our potential possibilities.

Victor Serebrakoff was fifteen years old when a high-school teacher told him he would never finish high school and that he should drop out and learn a trade. Victor, a restless boy by nature, took the advice and for the next seventeen years did a variety of odd jobs. He mowed lawns, bagged groceries and worked in a car wash.

A friend suggested to him, when he was thirty-two, that he had much more going for him than he realized. The friend encouraged him to take an IQ test at a nearby university in the city. Victor obliged and the resultant evaluation revealed that he was a genius with an IQ of 161.

Do you think he stayed at the car wash after the enlightening test? Not a chance. Instead, Victor started acting like a genius. He went to college and earned a degree. He secured a number of patents for inventions. He wrote several books and became a successful businessman.

This man's life changed as he viewed himself differently. He was, to some degree, the same person he was before the exam. And yet, because of his enhanced self-image, he was quite a different person.

Outside of sin itself, the greatest detriment to you becoming your best self is how you view yourself. The Bible says, in Proverbs 23:7 (KJV), "For as he thinketh in his heart, so is he." In other words, if you think you're junk, you'll act like junk.

You may treat yourself with disrespect. You may swallow and sniff things that were never meant to go into your body. You'll do things just because others pressure you to do it, not because you want to. You'll act in ways that will get you nowhere.

Two expressions are significant in regard to your perception of self. The terms *self-image* and *self-esteem* are often used interchangeably, but they're not the same. Your self-image is a reflection of what others have expressed to you over a lifetime and you've come to internalize it. It's who you think you are. Your self-esteem is how you feel about yourself or value yourself, based on who you think you are. Studies consistently demonstrate that eighty percent of us have a real struggle with self-esteem.

Developing Your Image

How do we get into this shape? Developmentally, our self-image comes about as infants. It's a feeling about our relationship to the world. It's called an image because we come to understand who we are as a reflection of what others tell us, for right or wrong.

Imagine, for a moment, what it would be like to be an infant once again. We were all there once. We've all been twenty inches long and weighed eight or nine pounds, looking out at the frighteningly huge world where we are totally dependent upon others. Even as we become ambulatory as toddlers, we're still the smallest human in the room. What does it feel like to stretch up to your full height and look somebody right in the… kneecap? You grow up in an intimidating world.

A group of sociologists in England built a scale model of a house from a small child's perspective. If a fully grown adult steps into the dining room, she discovers she can barely see the top of the table. She has to climb up into a chair. Reach up to turn the doorknob. Everything seems so big when you're a little child. This is how you viewed the world during your significant development years.

Also, consider the amount of correction a small child receives daily. Adults would be crushed if they had to endure the amount of criticism most children endure. Add older brothers and sisters into the mix and you've created a powerful recipe for a negative self-image. Since much of the human personality is in place by age six, this early view of ourselves "latches on" and becomes a big part of how we define ourselves.

Elementary school brings new feedback. The great social experiment of public school quickly offers us a whole different barrage of reflections on our worth, our capabilities and our attractiveness. You find out quickly if you're part of the "in" group socially, one of the smart ones academically or gifted ones athletically.

These assessments can cause a deep internal struggle. The grades, the nicknames, the shame of failures and even successes shape us. Some psychological scars from this period of your life stay with you. They're not visible to the human eye, but they're present.

Like rings within a tree that's been cut open, they offer a telling story. These could be called the wounds of childhood, impacting us as significantly as physical injuries.

I'm not suggesting that we all become beaten through these experiences. No, the human ego is amazingly resilient. It is true, though, that one's self-esteem does go up and down during this period of real adjustment in learning to live with people in society.

Then we explode into pubescence and enter the teenage years. What was the early period of adolescence like for you and your view of yourself? I guarantee you spent a fair amount of time gazing at your image in the mirror. You were likely criticized for spending too much time in the bathroom or giving an inordinate amount of attention to your hair or your makeup or your clothes.

It's a common malady of early puberty to take a great deal of time viewing what you're going to look like as you move into adulthood. There is a hypersensitivity to body awareness. Outwardly, you're asking, "Is this how I'm going to look all my life? Will I ever develop? Am I going to always be this body shape?" Inwardly, you're asking, "Who am I, really? What am I good at? Am I socially acceptable? Am I attractive? Do I like who I'm becoming?"

The thoughts come consistently in adolescence; your questions develop as fast as your body is growing. One boy, nearly twelve years old, was in a play celebrating America's Independence. In a classic Freudian slip, he cried out, "Give me puberty or give me death!" Sometimes, at that age, those seem like the only choices.

This is a traumatic time: it's especially hard on whatever sense of ego strength we may have developed over the first dozen or so years on this planet. Lyrics from an old John Lennon song, "Nobody told me there'd be days like these," describe every child in early pubescence.

I wasn't prepared to grow nine-and-one-half inches in a single year, documented month by month on the door frame of our kitchen entrance where we were measured. Acne, braces, the works—they all came my way. And this happens during a period of acute sensitivity. Our sense of self takes a real battering in the early teenage years because there's such a great emphasis on looks and most of us don't want to look like this all our lives.

Fortunately, we all pass through the teenage years and enter adulthood. But do questions regarding self continue? Absolutely. In fact, the pressure can be even greater. We still have great concerns about our worth, our attractiveness and usefulness, combined with a nagging sense that as adults, we ought to be able to do something about it.

Watch, at a playground, a little child who has a need for attention. He'll hang upside down on the monkey bars or stand up on the slide or swing high into the air and call out, "Look at me, Mommy! Look at me, Daddy!"

He's commanding attention. But more than that, he's seeking affirmation. He desires someone to say, "Oh—-you're wonderful! You're good at what you're doing. You're so clever."

Adults can't go around saying, "Look at me—look at me." That's not acceptable, so they do it in other ways. They say, more subtly,

See what part of town I live in?
Look at my shiny new car!
Wouldn't you love to have a slender body like mine?
Notice the ring I'm wearing...

People do this because, by the time you've reached adulthood, an image of yourself is entrenched in your mind. You think of yourself in a rather concretized manner. Alfred Adler used the phrase "inferiority complex" to describe the feelings of inadequacy many persons experience, no matter how successful they've become in life. They don't appreciate their God-given talents and abilities. It's as if there's a parent still standing over them, pointing a finger and saying, "That's not good enough, son. You'll have to do better, daughter."

19

Behind the crisp business suit of many an adult male is often an awkward adolescent still trying to prove himself to the boys or show off for the girls. Underneath that woman's lovely, stylish dress is really a timid little girl, still wondering what others think of her. Day after day, physically attractive, intelligent people dance across the TV screen with the right comeback, the perfect skin and the ability to solve all their pressing problems in a one-minute commercial or a twenty-two minute sitcom. The television simply reinforces feelings of inadequacy.

Hoping to Cope

So, how do most persons cope with this sagging insecurity over self-esteem? One major area in which we attempt to store up emotional ammunition against the world is through physical appearance. The appeal in all the advertisements is that if you look good and smell nice, you'll feel confident. As a result, we run out and make sure we purchase the products that will ensure these feelings. However, this is just veneer over the surface. Confidence is an inner matter. Job said, "Let not him that is deceived trust in vanity: for vanity shall be his recompence."[1]

A second means of coping involves what Freud termed "the herd instinct." Fit into a crowd dressed like those around you. Don't stick out. Merge your identity with that of a group. If they all wear baggy pants, wear baggy pants. If they shave their heads, whip out the razor and shaving cream.

This "herd" coping style works as long as you're surrounded by a group of like-minded individuals. Remove the crowd and take the support away, and your sense of identity crashes with it.

Others cope through achievement, tangible vestiges of success, degrees earned, a corner office, a title, financial success or contests won. These may, of course, build your sense of personal esteem for a while, but they are all transient. Money comes and goes. Today's success is forgotten tomorrow. Titles change hands.

The Bible has much to say to the issue of self-image that all of us struggle with to an extent. Putting the various verses together, there are three great thoughts to assist you in your quest:

1) Realize whose you are.

2) Realize where you're going.

3) Realize what's important.

Whose You Are

First, realize whose you are, not who you are. You only come to understand who you are in relation to whose you are. You are God's. You're created in the image of God. As recorded in Genesis, when God had finished the various parts of His Creation, He said it was good. Upon completing a man and a woman, He declared it was very good. Human beings are the highlight of God's creation. We are "fearfully and wonderfully made." Isaiah wrote "Look to the rock from which you were cut and to the quarry from which you were hewn"[2] You're a very special person. You are God's son or daughter, claimed by God even before your conception.

God loves you so dearly that He allowed His Son to come and live upon this earth and have His life cruelly snapped out, so that He would rise again to set us at peace with God. Paul reminds us in his first letter to the Corinthians, "For you were bought at a price; therefore glorify God in your body and in your spirit, which are God's."[3]

Christ died for you. To not love yourself or to be upset with your natural features is to lay a charge against God. It's saying, "God, You made a mistake. You didn't do a good enough job when

You made me." To have a healthy sense of self is to be able to say, "Thank You, God. It's good to be me. I'm pleased to be me. I appreciate who I am and whose I am."

Where Are You Going, Anyway?

When you are secure in knowing whose you are, the self you were meant to be begins to unfold as you unlock your potential. Often this is like a jump-start or a re-start to latent talents and desires long buried.

Dr. Carol Gilligan has reported that there is a stronger sense of self-esteem in girls until about the age of ten. Then, somewhere in the pre-adolescent years between ten to thirteen, something happens. They seem to lose touch with their inner voice, their sense of identity and strength.

In school, they begin to "dummy up." That is, the girls realize boys are threatened by females who are too intelligent or ambitious. How does the "dummying up" play itself out? She'll be careful not to look too aggressive. She may know the answer in class, but won't raise her hand. She'll opt for safe things—worry about applying eyeliner instead of applying her IQ; have concern about clothes instead of career; make safe decisions. Settle for being the nurse instead of the physician. Become a legal clerk instead of a lawyer.

Now it doesn't matter whether you're male or female—you can always find an excuse. You can always blame your environment, your grades, your race, your physical stature or your school.

The real question to ask, though, is not where have you been, but where are you going? The reason that's such an important question is because your goals determine what you will do to get to that place.

The Road Yet to be Traveled

This is your new chapter of the family history. It is your time to decide, with God's guidance, where you are to go. When you look at life with a new perspective, with an enhanced sense of self, what do you hope will happen in the future?

Hope is critical because it shapes you. It focuses your goals, your efforts, your very life. It's making a tough choice, a decision to break away from the pack. Teenage years are typically the "group years." You hear the term *peer pressure* until you could gag, but it's true—you're tuned into group values. The further one moves into adulthood, the more personal values you claim for yourself.

- Will I be an overcomer, or an underachiever?
- Will I be held back with the group, or move ahead with my life?
- Am I going to live with self-imposed limits, or am I going to smoke out those old boundaries?

It was once written that, "When you make your mark in the world, look out for the guys with erasers." It's your call. Will you let others erase your future plans and hopes, or will you and God make the call?

The trick is believing what you can be, especially when it seems to take so long. I read once about the Chinese bamboo tree, an unusual tree that seems to hardly grow at all for the first four years; then, suddenly during the fifth year, it shoots up ninety feet in just sixty days. Would you say that bamboo tree grew up in sixty days or five years? The answer is *both*. It's a process.

Life is a lot like the bamboo tree. Sometimes it seems like you keep putting forth more and more effort, day after day and nothing seems to happen. No growth. No progress.

Yet for those who persevere, there's a reward coming. One day you bear fruit. You shoot up in maturity. You attain some of your goals. It all starts to come together.

This is putting perspiration into your aspirations. Theodore Roosevelt once claimed, "I'm an average man, but I work at it harder than the average man." There are few things in life more gratifying than reaching a long sought-after goal.

Pay Attention to Priorities

Finally, in coming to understand and appreciate yourself, realize what's important. In Luke's Gospel, we read, "what is highly esteemed among men is an abomination in the sight of God."[4]

The priorities of men and women are not the same as the priorities of God. God says,

> For my thoughts are not your thoughts, neither are your
> ways my ways…. As the heavens are higher than the earth,
> so are my ways higher than your ways and my thoughts
> than your thoughts.[5]

What is important? Are looks really as essential as our culture tries to tell us and the media attempts to sell us? The Bible describes Jesus as not being comely, so perhaps He really wasn't that handsome fellow portrayed in artists' renditions. Nor was the apostle Paul very good-looking. Tradition tells us he was a small, wiry fellow with a big hawk-nose. He probably couldn't see very well either.

The Proverbs 31 account of what a great wife would be like has many details, with one glaring absence: physical beauty. In fact, the second-to-last verse of the chapter adds, "Charm is deceptive, and beauty is fleeting; but a woman who fears the LORD is to be praised."[6]

This, of course, doesn't mean you don't take care of yourself; far from it. Your body is the temple of God. It just means you don't value persons for how they appear. You've got the family nose, ears that stick out, thin hair, too short or too tall—it's not that important.

What is important is *You*—the person who lives inside this body for a number of years. *You*—a special person in God's sight, loved and cherished.

We're eternally beating our heads against a wall if we keep trying to understand who we are outside of our relationship to God. We truly discover *who* we are as we come to grips with *whose* we are.

We are forlorn like children and experienced like old men. We are crude and sorrowful and superficial—I believe we are lost.

—ERICH MARIA REMARQUE,
from *All Quiet on the Western Front*

O God, our souls are restless until they find their repose in thee.

—ST. AUGUSTINE

Whoever finds his life will lose it and whoever loses his life for my sake will find it.

—JESUS CHRIST (MATTHEW 10:39, NIV)

Fear not that your life shall come to an end, but rather that it shall never have a beginning.

—ANONYMOUS

Sin can bring pleasure but never happiness.

—R.C. SPROUL

How long will you love worthlessness and seek falsehood?

—PSALM 4:2B, NKJV

America is said to have the highest per capita boredom of any spot on earth! We know that because we have the greatest variety and greatest number of artificial amusements of any country. People have become so empty that they can't even entertain themselves. They have to pay other people to amuse them, to make them laugh, to try to make them feel warm and happy and comfortable for a few minutes, to try to lose that awful, frightening, hollow feeling—that terrible, dreaded feeling of being lost and alone.

—BILLY GRAHAM

What Am I Looking For?

"Get a life..."

*R*estless people. Everywhere I go, I see restless people. Walking places, driving places, going to school, to jobs, to shopping centers. Buying the latest gadget. Trying the newest hairstyle. Hunting for a new romance. Searching for activities that will relieve them from the monotony and boredom of their lives.

Where does this drive come from, anyway? What are people really looking for?

Right now we could be described as a society in search of itself. People are groping, searching, stretching and testing the very limits of law and life itself. Commenting on this search, Billy Graham said, "Some of you are good only because you can't afford to be bad."

I think he was right. Most of you have daydreamed about all you would do if you won the lottery or became independently wealthy, and no doubt most of it would be directed towards meeting your needs. Just imagine if you could have all your heart desired! Would it be good for you? In the whimsical words of comedian Steven Wright, "You can't have everything! Where would you put it?"

Solomon, the likely author of Ecclesiastes, was a person who restlessly sought out to explore all of life and had it all. If there was ever a human being for whom the slogan "you only go around once in life, grab all the gusto you can" was appropriate, it was Solomon. Yet, at the beginning of Ecclesiastes, he declares: "Meaningless! Meaningless!... Utterly meaningless! Everything is meaningless" (Ecclesiastes 1:2). He proclaims the ancient version of "been there, done that," by saying,

All things are wearisome,
more than one can say.
The eye never has enough of seeing,
Nor the ear its fill of hearing,
What has been will be again,
What has been done will be done again,
There is nothing new under the sun
(Ecclesiastes 1:8–9, NIV).

Solomon decided to search out all that was under the sun to see if it would abate his inner longing—no holds barred. You'll surely identify with all of these drives.

Pleasure

Solomon gave himself to all the pleasure available to a human being. In his heart, he thought "I'll test you with pleasure to find out what's good" (2:1).

He tried laughter and fun (2:2). No doubt he surrounded himself with the most humorous and fun people of his day. A good time, parties and lots of laughter can bring joy for a while—then you're left flat. "Foolish," Solomon eventually surmised. For every high of a party, eventually you have to come down. Laughter is hollow when the rest of one's life is absent of joy.

28

So, Solomon tried cheering himself with alcohol (2:3). Drinking a lot of wine certainly dulls the senses and relieves inhibitions for a while—and then there's the return to reality.

Solomon then attempted to find pleasure in beautiful buildings and gardens and art (2:4–6). There surely can be much beauty in such efforts. Visit any large city in the world and you'll see an abundance of projects much like those undertaken by Solomon. Yet, for all they add to our lives, they can quickly become an end in themselves. Look at how many people live to create and cultivate a beautiful house and sculptured lawn at the expense of what gives life real meaning. I call this an "edifice complex," for there always seems to be a need for a bigger house, or a better lawn or a fresh renovation.

My wife and I once observed how many younger couples we knew who divorced shortly after building their dream house. Apparently, the much greater attention had been given to building a house and not a home.

Solomon then tested out purchasing power. No credit cards needed—he went shopping (2:7). He amassed more stuff than anyone did in his city before him. In a slave-holding society, he could even buy people, which he did so in abundance.

Perhaps you've heard or read the statement, "when the going gets tough, the tough go shopping." How easy and exciting it is to whip out a credit card and purchase those new clothes or that hairstyle or tattoo or gadget. And how equally the newness wears off. I had a three-year period in which I owned and sold seven different cars and two motorcycles. It was also the unhappiest time in my adult life, for somehow I had bought into the illusion that buying things would make me feel better.

Solomon also leaned towards music, just like many of you (2:8). Music is a wonderful part of life. Moreover, he was a musician, and as a musician he wrote over 1005 songs (1 Kings 4:32). The best men and women singers of the day performed for him, but eventually the notes fell flat as they only filled in the gaps for a while.

Solomon even had a harem (2:8). Hundreds of women were at his disposal. All the sex, in any variety, at any time—a fantasy for many people in our sex-saturated society. Solomon lived the dream. He had "all the delights of the heart of man."

In his own words he claimed:

I denied myself nothing my eyes desired,
I refused my heart no pleasure.
My heart took delight in all my work
And this was the reward for all my labor.
Yet when I surveyed all that my hands had done
And what I had toiled to achieve,
Everything was meaningless, a chasing after the wind;
Nothing was gained under the sun (2:10–11, NIV).

This is not to knock pleasure. Later he calls it the gift of God. He writes that it's good to eat and drink and enjoy the good of all your labor (5:18). But it is "pleasure for a season," as it is transient and temporary. Pleasure-seeking can become all encompassing and demanding. It can become addictive. We can become prisoners of our appetites.

In fourteenth-century Belgium, two brothers vied for a throne and a dukedom. Raynold, the older brother, nicknamed Crassus (Latin for "fat"), was defeated by his younger brother, Edward.

Edward had a room built around Raynold in the Nieuwkerk Castle and said he would give up his title when his fat brother could leave the room. The room had several windows and a normal-sized door, but Raynold was too large to get out. Furthermore, each day Edward had Raynold's favorite foods, pastries and appetizers sent to him daily, knowing his older brother had little willpower. Eventually, Raynold grew heavier all the still and stayed in that room for ten years, until Edward died in a fierce battle. Raynold died within a year of being released, his health irreparably harmed by his own appetites.

I once saw rock musician Eric Clapton being interviewed on television. He described his life as a rock superstar: fame, money, sex, alcohol and drugs were his daily companions. He even stole away Beatle George Harrison's wife. With all that he had, he claimed his life was miserable. Nearly every day he contemplated suicide. He was in drug rehabilitation twice. With the world at his feet, Clapton was depressed and despondent.

The occasion of the interview was the celebration of ten years being clean and sober. He had helped raise seven million dollars for a drug rehabilitation center in Aruba. Clapton affirmed that life used to be in black and white, and now it was in technicolor.

Solomon would understand:

> I have seen another evil under the sun, and it weighs heavily on men: God gives a man wealth, possessions and honor, so that he lacks nothing his heart desires, but God does not enable him to enjoy them… (Ecclesiastes 6:1–2a, NIV).

Robert Frink, a man in Austin, Minnesota, legally changed his name to "Welcome Pleasure Freely." The judge granted his request with a word of caution: "Don't expect an easy time getting a check cashed."

Pleasure is a check that never cashes in. We have more pleasure-producing devices than any time before in history. We have our radios and compact discs as constant companions; a hundred choices on our cable television. We can shop around the clock. Yet we still haven't learned the lesson of the Bible, that pleasure is fleeting and temporary.

Wisdom

Solomon then set his sights on wisdom (1:16,17). This would seem to be a worthy goal. I mean, after all, what could possibly be wrong with seeking after wisdom? The answer: Generally nothing. Solomon became the wisest man who ever lived. He spoke 3000 proverbs (1 Kings 4:32), and people hung on his every word.

Knowledge can puff up, however. Much learning can lead to much vanity and pride.

Having spent most of my adult life studying and teaching at American colleges and universities, I can tell you there is plenty of pride. Some of the finest, open thinkers I know hold doctorates in their fields. There are many with doctorates who believe they are broad-minded persons when, in fact, their thoughts and presuppositions about life are quite narrow, rigid and shallow. I've seen it time and time again on college campuses.

John Wesley was one of the most brilliant minds of Western civilization. His achieved grade point average at Oxford University is still unequaled nearly three hundred years since his matriculation. Wesley was immediately offered a professorship upon graduation, which he accepted.

Then, this great thinker had a genuine encounter with God and "his heart was strangely warmed." His philosophy changed quite dramatically and he wrote that the rest of his life he wanted to study the wisdom found in the Bible. Wesley said, "Let me be a man of one book. O' give me that book."

I once heard a speaker describe his ministry on a college campus. One of the ministries was a Bible study for college men. A young man in the study came to visit him one afternoon with an announcement. This student was tired of being a Christian. He was observing other university students who partied, cheated and slept around, and he was fed up with all the moral restrictions that came along with Christianity. He said he'd be back eventually, but for the rest of the school year, he was just going to give vent to his passions like many others were doing.

The campus minister replied, "Fine. It's your choice. I may not like it, but it's your life and I won't stop you. First, though, let me leave you with a Bible verse to think on." Looking at the student squarely in the eyes, he quoted:

> Be happy, young man, while you are young,
> and let your heart give you joy in the days of your youth.
> Follow the ways of your heart
> and whatever your eyes see,
> but know that for all these things
> God will bring you to judgment.[1]

The college student looked at him a minute and said, "OK… see ya 'round." For three weeks, he was nowhere to be seen. One day, he showed up before the Bible study. He looked miserable.

The leader said, "You look pretty bad." The student nodded his head. "I *feel* pretty bad. I've had an awful last three weeks. There's just one thing I want to know. Where is that Bible verse you quoted to me? It haunted me day and night whenever I tried to do anything wrong."

The verse is in Ecclesiastes 11:9. Solomon wrote it. The words and wisdom of the Bible contain power for our lives and can instruct, convict and heal.

Wealth

Solomon then turned his attention to the accumulation of wealth. He owned the finest palace. Servants waited on him hand and foot. The Queen of Sheba was astonished at his wealth. He became the wealthiest man on the face of the earth. After obtaining all that, Solomon was moved to write, "He that loveth silver shall not be satisfied with silver; nor he that loveth abundance with increase" (5:10, KJV).

He came to realize that the accumulation of wealth by itself can never make a person happy. Not only that, everything is left behind when we die. There are no U-Hauls following the hearse.

> As he came forth of his mother's womb, naked shall he return to go as he came, and shall take nothing of his labour, which he may carry away in his hand (5:15, KJV).

When Wal-Mart founder Sam Walton died, a friend mused about how much money he left behind. I said that I knew exactly how much he left. All of it. Every penny. You can't take it with you to the other side. As Shakespeare wrote, "...or sells eternity to get a toy, many give away their souls for the accumulation of wealth on earth."

Someone has said that the best things in life are not things. Money really can't buy you happiness. Luke 12:15 records that Jesus once said, "A man's life does not consist in the abundance of his possessions." In detailed studies done in the United States and Europe, the wealthiest parts of the globe, there was little correlation found between income and happiness. In fact, rapid increases in wealth resulted in less, not more, happiness.

A lot of people think if they could win the lottery or inherit a million dollars, they'd be happy. As a general rule, it doesn't seem to be true at all.

Religion

Finally, Solomon tried religion. In the Book of 2 Chronicles, chapters 6 to 9, the story is told of the dedication of Solomon's famous temple. It was a glittering place of worship created by thousands of craftsmen. Twenty-two thousand oxen and one-hundred-twenty thousand sheep and goats were given in sacrifice on the altar to God. It was history's biggest barbecue, followed by fifteen days of feasting and rejoicing.

All of Solomon's many other accomplishments paled in comparison to this great act of building a house to worship God. And with all the glory and excitement of this, it wasn't enough.

He'd fulfilled all his religious duty. He'd honored God—and his father, David—through this building. He'd done all the right things.

Yet, religion alone never ultimately answers the searching heart. A Muslim has a religion. A Buddhist has a religion. Someone has described religion as men and women looking for God. One can have a religion and still not know and experience God.

The contrast of Christianity is that God comes down, in the form of Jesus Christ, looking for men and women. Christianity is about a relationship, not a religion. Solomon tried religion, and it came up short. It always will.

What did this great man come to realize, after pursuing wealth, wisdom, pleasure—even religion? It was all without meaning if one didn't live rightly in relationship to God. He concluded his thought by writing, "Let us hear the conclusion of the whole matter: Fear God, and keep his commandments: for this is the whole duty of man" (12:13). Fearing God is a healthy kind of fear. It's recognizing your place, your plan; the very meaning of your existence is rooted in God. To keep God's commandments means to live within the boundaries in which life is to be experienced at its greatest depth of joy and purpose.

Jesus Christ once asked two men this most fundamental of all questions: "What are you looking for?"[2] It's a most relevant question for you and me. Jesus' unique answer was to come and see. God first reaches out to us, and then we're offered the opportunity to respond. We're not forced into this. We're to come and see and then decide.

You might ask yourself that question—what are you looking for? The actions of your life will tell on you. Here are some possibilities:

- discover yourself
- have fun
- get attention
- gain power
- be loved
- being seen as smart
- make money
- be at peace
- have a career
- (*insert your own search here*)
- seeking God (*right answer*)

The wisdom of sages like Solomon echoes to us down the halls of eternity. The internal search in which we are all a part is a matter of the soul. And thus, the answer for this meaning can only be found in God.

If you have sight, you are blessed.
If you have insight, you are a thousand times blessed.

—UNKNOWN

The universe is a stairway leading nowhere unless man is immortal.

—EDGAR YOUNG MULLINS

If success is not on your own terms; if it looks good to the world but does not feel good in your heart, it is not success at all.

—ANNA QUINDLEN

Know that the Lord is God.
It is he who made us, and we are his.

—PSALM 100:3A, NIV

The destined end of man is not happiness nor health, but holiness. God's one aim is the production of saints. He is not an eternal blessing machine for men. He did not come to save men out of pity; He came to save men because He had created them to be holy.

—OSWALD CHAMBERS

Yesterday is but a dream; tomorrow is only a vision. But today well lived makes every yesterday a dream of happiness, and every tomorrow a vision of hope.

—ANCIENT PROVERB

Alice: Would you tell me please, which way I ought to go from here?
Cheshire Cat: That depends a good deal on where you want to get to.

—LEWIS CARROLL'S *Alice in Wonderland*

What's Really Real?

"Reality check"

*g*uess I knew it would come to this. In a celebrity-mad culture, you can become a celebrity for a day for the price of an admissions ticket. There are now theme parks which let you be a star for an evening. You pay fifty dollars in advance, then show up at the main gate with your admissions card on your designated evening. A crowd presses up to see you; photographers take pictures; reporters try to interview you; teenage girls scream and call out your name.

During your meal, a tuxedo-clad gentleman comes over and says he's writing a movie screenplay with you in mind. Before the night is over, you've been edited into a movie scene with real stars of the screen. Wow, what a rush! And the theme parks have been playing to capacity crowds. You may think these participants have way too much time on their hands, but stop and think for a moment: what does its popularity say about people and our culture?

Things Aren't Always as They Appear to Be

We understand, first of all, *people aren't all they appear to be*. Inside each of us is an inner child yearning for attention and desiring to have significance. There is a whole other person beneath the surface.

There is that hidden self, which some might call the real self. It is the part of you that perhaps you have to suppress to adapt to your job, your position, your family. Many times I have talked with individuals in the counseling room who felt stifled within because they couldn't express who they really were. They felt a yearning to express who they really are.

Secondly, *situations aren't all they appear to be*. The apostle Paul asks if we assess situations by their outward appearance; that is, what we see only by our physical eyesight![1]

In Christianity, the horror of the crucifixion was a prelude to the resurrection. Situations may appear negative when often they're just window dressing to a greater opportunity in life.

There was a very elderly woman who had experienced a great deal of trials in her life. In spite of all the difficulties, she maintained a sunny, optimistic disposition towards life. She was once asked how she managed so well despite all her problems. She smiled and answered, "When Christ died, it looked bad for three days. Then on the third day He arose. So, now when I have a trial, I just tell myself, 'wait three days,' and it always turns out so much for the better."

The difficulty of a situation is always relative to how bad you think it is for you. For example, thousands of whining Christians have been transformed by short-term mission trips to an impoverished nation where they saw how much worse it could be. Just a couple of short weeks gave them much greater appreciation for their lives back home.

As I write this, economists are lamenting how bad an economic downturn could become. It just made me laugh. (Harry Truman said he wished for a one armed economist to advise him, so the man wouldn't always be saying "on the other hand.") The United States lives in a luxury unparalleled by the rest of the world.

Peggy Noonan has eloquently written about why we are so

unhappy when we have it so good.[2] How many people in the world could only dream of living within the safety and wealth of American borders? You've heard it said that *imitation* is the most sincere form of flattery. I'd suggest *immigration* is the most sincere form.

We have it so good, which leads to another point. *The world isn't all it appears to be.* The apostle Paul once wrote that "we see through a glass darkly."[3]

We will never fully understand all that goes on around us in the world.

The Bible describes this earth as a spiritual battleground. It would be easy to look at the world and feel like caving in. There is much hatred, racism, apathy, unkindness and war across the globe.

Despite how ugly things may appear, let me put a positive Biblical spin on this. Have you ever wondered why, wherever Jesus went, He encountered demonic activity? Read through the four Gospels and right and left, there were demons manifesting all around Jesus, the Son of God. Wherever He appears, demonic activity is stepped up.

Here is a deep spiritual truth. Whenever demonic activity increases, it means the Son of God is near, not far away. In the past several years, there has been an enormous increase of demonic activity:

- witchcraft
- occult, psychics
- horrific movies
- pornography
- insane murders, mass killings

It might be possible to interpret this as God deserting us. Not so. God is nearer than you think. Whenever evil activity is stepped up, the Son of God will soon appear. Don't judge the world by present appearances.

Reality Check

If it's true, then, that people, situations and the world itself are not all as they appear to be, what we need is a better grasp on what is real: a reality check.

Where are we going to get a reality check? Don't trust Hollywood or the media. A clever, anonymous writer once described reality according to Hollywood. He wrote:

- The Eiffel Tower can be seen from any window in Paris

- Cars that crash almost always burst into flames

- It's always possible to park directly outside the building you are visiting

- A man will show no pain while taking the most ferocious beating, but will wince when a woman tries to clean his wounds

- All bombs are fitted with electronic timing devices with large red readouts so you know exactly when they will go off

- (*My favorite*) It doesn't matter if you are heavily outnumbered in a fight involving martial arts—your enemies will patiently wait to attack you, one by one, dancing around in a threatening manner until you have knocked out their predecessors.[4]

That may be Hollywood's version of reality, but it's not real. Neither is the world of public school. Its there to prepare you for life as an educated person and it may or may not succeed in the task because it is a temporary, artificial atmosphere.

Ann Landers once passed on an article with ten rules for the real world that you don't learn in school. It's a good message and worth repeating, even though it was primarily directed to teenagers:

Life is not fair. Get used to it. The average teenager uses the phrase "It's not fair" eighty-six times a day.

The real world won't care as much about your self-esteem as your school does.

Sorry, you won't make $40,000 a year as soon as you get out of high school. You might even have to wear a uniform that doesn't have a designer label on it.

If you think your teacher is tough, wait until you get a boss.

Flipping burgers is not beneath your dignity. Your grand-parents had a different word for burger flipping—they called it "opportunity."

It's not your parent's fault if you mess up. You're responsible.

Before you were born, your parents weren't boring. They got that way by paying bills and listening to you.

Life is not divided into semesters. You don't get summers off. You are expected to show up every day for eight hours, and you don't get a new life every ten weeks.

Smoking does not look cool. Watch an eleven-year-old with a butt in his mouth. That's what you look like to anyone over twenty.

Your school may be "outcome-based," but life isn't. In some schools, you're given as many chances as you want to get the answer right. This, of course, bears not the slightest resemblance to anything in real life—as you will soon find out.

I once knew a young man named Farley who, since his mid-teens, had lived in a psychiatric ward. He struggled with schizophrenia, a mental disorder marked by loss of contact with reality. Every day, a hundred times or more, Farley would utter the phrase, "It's real, it's real…" as if to remind himself what was real and what were hallucinations.

Many people are spiritually schizophrenic. They have lost control with the ultimate source reality and thereby live a life of delusions and half-truths. Perhaps we could better understand what is real by asking—what *isn't* real? The Bible lets us know anything that captures our attention more than God isn't eternally real. These are referred to as "the little foxes that spoil the vineyard." Your vineyard, your life, becomes spoiled, and you don't become a fruitful person.

Also, that which takes more time than God isn't eternally real. Countless persons have become convinced their fulfillment, their job, their plans, were more real than God. Time spent at the office was viewed as infinitely more important than prayer and communication with God.

That which exalts itself above God is not eternally real, either. This was the core sin. It was the sin of Satan: pride.

Have you ever noticed people who act so important now won't always be in a position of power? Someday, they'll be forgotten. People come and go over time.

When I had been in the Army about a year, I was promoted to acting sergeant. I wasn't eligible to be promoted to sergeant, so I was what was called "an acting jack." I was actually given orders and had the stripes put on so I could order a platoon of men around.

I was a good soldier. I worked hard, looked sharp, my uniform was creased and my boots shone like glass, but I wasn't really a sergeant yet. I knew it down deep and that kept me humble and in right relationship with my men. It was a temporary position, so I stayed in touch with the reality of who I really was.

Nothing, absolutely nothing, can be allowed to exalt itself over God. Henri Nouwen is one of my examples in life. Now deceased, this Catholic priest was once a professor at Harvard—a wonderful writer and speaker. In fact, he realized that, because of his gifts and popularity, he was becoming a kind of celebrity cult-figure. Elvis Christian. So he dropped it all. He left all of this for the mission field in Bolivia.

There, he lived in an earthen hut with a dirt floor. After five years, he returned to North America, settling in Canada and spending the last eleven years of his life working at a home for severely mentally handicapped people in Toronto, where he lovingly ministered to people who could never be impressed by his books, degrees or any of the useful skills he'd learned over the years. He claimed it was like starting his life all over again. He no longer was dependent on any of his past positions.

Henri Nouwen had discovered a secret hidden from most of us. Reality is in the presence of God. It's real, because what you do about your relationship with God determines eternity.

- Real is loving God with all your heart.
- Real is loving your neighbor as yourself
- Real is a life of self-sacrifice
- Real is having forgiveness and cleansing in your life because a God-man died on a cross 2,000 years ago and shed His blood to forgive you.

This is a reality check and it changes how you think, forever.

A New Point of View

A fifth-grade class was asked by their teacher to count the number of stars they could see that night in the sky. It was a clear night and all the students had fun counting stars. The next day the reports came in—

Jason counted 184;
Susan saw 165;
Mark's tally was 98.

One boy didn't say anything, so the teacher asked, "Russell, how many stars did you count last night?" Russell answered, "Three." "But Russell," the teacher protested, "how come you only saw three stars when everyone else counted so many?" His answer came quickly: "Teacher, we have a small backyard."

This is a problem for most of us. Our view of reality, our view of the universe, is too small. We need to have a new point of view.

The Bible presents Jesus Christ as being the most real person there ever was. The Greek word for real, *alethenos*, is closely related to the word *alethes*, which means "true." Over and over again, Gospel writers claim that Jesus is the real (true) light, the real (true) bread and the real (true) vine. Reality is never clearer than when looking into the personhood of Jesus Christ.

When one comes to a place of faith in Jesus Christ, when the love of God seeps into your soul, as a new creation, you gain a new point of view. You see yourself differently. Jesus said we are made clean by the word He spoke to us.

Let's use an analogy. Can you think of a time when you were really, really dirty? Maybe you'd worked on a filthy job and couldn't wait to scrub up and be clean before rejoining the human race. At age seventeen, I got a summer job at the best-paying factory in town. It was a seafood and onion ring factory. Boy, did it smell! I'd arrive for the eleven p.m. shift, and all night long I'd climb in and out of machines as I cleaned them. I couldn't wait to get home after completing my tasks at seven a.m. I would be absolutely filthy. I would scrub and shower for the longest time. I would double check with family and friends and make sure I smelled okay. It felt so good to be clean. It was like being reborn.

That is similar to what happens on a spiritual level. When God makes you clean, you're really clean. Forgiven. God chooses to remember your sin no more. As far as the east is from the west, your sins are removed from your life.

And maybe it's difficult to believe. You inquire of friends and others as to whether you're really okay. You're still inhabiting the same body. You can still see evidences of a past life, of past transgressions. And you might just start to stagger a bit in your faith and listen to thoughts of doubt within.

Recently, I talked on the telephone with a lovely person I've known for some time, who lives in shaky marriage with an unkind, unfaithful husband. She has been a Christian for several years now, a new creation. She said that in all her years of marriage, she'd never, ever received a Valentine card from her husband. In response I told her, just spontaneously, "Oh, you're such a wonderful person. We think so highly of you. You deserve a Valentine!" and she started crying over the phone. She's a new creature in God. God has made her a beautiful, strong person. Some people in her life may not validate this yet, but God does.

Do you know that when God looks at you, it's with eyes of love? God says, "You're wonderful—you deserve a Valentine."

This is seeing yourself from a new point of view—seeing yourself from God's perspective. Perhaps you protest that you stumble. Your make mistakes. You sin. You fall. *Of course* you do. Yet, think about this: if you were the parent of a toddler, you'd totally accept that a little child falls down a lot. You wouldn't say, "Hey, get up, you dumb kid! You're almost fourteen months old! You should be walking better than that. What's the matter with you?"

Of course not. You'd pick up that child when he falls down. You'd caress the child. You'd kiss her sweet, sweaty little forehead. You'd hold on to those soft little chubby fingers and help your toddler walk again. That's exactly how God looks at us—with loving patience. With mercy and grace and kindness. With tenderness.

This is what is really real. God is there to help you along as you mature and make your mark on this world.

Most people creep into the world and know no reason why they're born except to consume the corn and fish and leave behind an empty dish.

—ISAAC WATTS

He has spent all his life letting down empty buckets into empty wells and he's frittering away his age trying to draw them up again.

—SYDNEY SMITH, SPEAKING OF A FRIEND

What can a man give in exchange for his soul?

—JESUS CHRIST (MARK 8:37, NIV)

The noblest question in the world is, "what good may I do in it?"

—BENJAMIN FRANKLIN

The great use of a life is to spend it for something that outlasts it.

—WILLIAM JONES

Here is a test to see if your mission on earth is finished. If you're alive, it isn't.

—FRANCIS BACON

I shall pass through this world but once. Any good I can do, or any kindness that I can show any human being, let me do it now and not defer it. For I shall not pass this way again.

—STEPHEN GRELLET

Into What Will I Invest My Life?

"The fingerprint you leave behind..."

*W*hat do St. Francis, Abraham Lincoln, Clara Barton and John Lennon all have in common? Answer: They're all dead. Death comes to us all. It is the final stop sign for life's journey.

Because it happens to all of us, the Bible reminds us to soberly consider our time on earth. The psalmist wrote, "Teach us to number our days aright, that we may gain a heart of wisdom."[1]

A similar thought has been suggested by Stephen Covey. He says, "To begin with the end in mind." In other words, consider your life as you'd liked to have lived it when you reach the end.

There was a true occurrence witnessed by a minister and his wife at a swimming pool in England a number of years ago. As they were sitting at poolside, a striking, muscular young man strode into the pool area. He caught everyone's attention as he walked to the pool edge near the diving board and gingerly put his toe into the water in much the same manner as a child. He next climbed to the highest diving board, raised his arms high and performed a beautiful dive into the water with hardly a splash. The young man swam to the edge of the pool and plopped down not far from the clergy couple.

The minister's curiosity was aroused. "Excuse me, sir" he said. "Forgive me for being so inquisitive, but how is it you started out just now as such a novice and ended like such an expert?"

The young man smiled sheepishly. "It's a long story, really. I'm a schoolteacher at a boys' school. One hot, sticky night, I decided to take a swim about ten in the evening.

"I went to the highest diving board and put my arms above my head to dive when... across the surface of the pool, a shadow of a cross appeared as the moon shone through the trees.

"I watched, fascinated, until it went away. I again raised my arms to dive, when the same shadow appeared, and with it, I had the strongest urge not to dive. I climbed down and went to the pool's edge to get a better look at the shadow. I discovered, to my horror, that the pool had been drained. It was bone dry. If I'd have dived, I'd been killed outright. That's why I can never swim before checking to make sure the water's really there. I guess you could say it was the cross that saved me."

Stop and think for a moment of a time when *your* life was spared. A split second, a near miss, an illness treated early enough, perhaps as a result of your being very careful, or hypersensitive or even fearful of certain situations. "For death is the destiny of every man; the living should take this to heart" (Ecclesiastes 7:2b, NIV).

But no matter what you do, it's one-hundred percent certain that someday your legacy on earth will be complete. Don't dwell on it, though, until it becomes a morbid thought. Let it motivate you. So, what will you invest your life in now to create that legacy? The military refers to this as the "mission essential task." You didn't know it at the time, but it was God who spared your life. It was the merciful purpose of Christ to set you aside to be saved by the cross—in this life and the next. Since we're all going to die, why not die for something worthwhile?

Welcome to What's Next

Saints of old knew this truth. One of the rules St. Benedict, one of the founders of monasticism, lived by was, day by day remind yourself that you are going to die.

In the popular *Tuesdays with Morrie*, by Mitch Alborn, there's a place where Morrie Schwartz, a slowly dying mentor, says,

> Everyone knows they're going to die... but nobody believes it. If we did, we would do things differently. There's a better approach. To know you're going to die and to be prepared for it at any time. That's better. That way you can actually be more involved in your life while living.[2]

Here is the impetus for even thinking about dying someday. It can make you think more about living right now and making a lasting contribution.

It's easy to mix things up. Some can malign this good thought by living too much in the future. In an anonymous and sad bit of prose that came my way once, the author wrote:

> First I was dying to finish high school and start college.
> And then I was dying to finish college and start working.
> And then I was dying to marry and have children.
> And then I was dying for my children to grow old enough for school so I could return to work.
> And then I was dying to retire.
> And now, I am dying... and suddenly I realize I forgot to live.

Theologian Paul Tillich once wrote about his belief that three fears accompany the human condition. The three were fear about meaninglessness, fear about death, and fear about guilt. Whether he was right or not is not that important. I am convinced, though, if one lives with real meaning and faces death as part of life, then there will be little guilt. We'll be too busy living and fulfilling our God-given purpose on earth with joy in our hearts.

Others may focus too much in the past to avoid the present and the future.

John Burroughs put it well:

In sorrow he learned the truth—
One may return to the place of his birth,
He cannot go back to his youth.

Lincoln said, "You cannot escape the responsibility of tomorrow by evading it today."

A recent death of a member of my larger Army command underscored this truth. Under the influence of alcohol, a thirty-two year-old sergeant died accidentally in a swimming pool. For the eulogy, the chaplain from the unit searched over the deceased's too-brief life history to discover, in thirty-two years of living, the man had fathered nine children by nine different women—and he never raised a single child. This was his legacy as his past was laid bare: a series of affairs and nine precious human beings brought into this world, rejected by their father.

Instead of becoming a mature, responsible man, the sergeant was still sowing his seeds well into adulthood. How sad.

The past can't be undone. The future is yet to be lived, and it's yours for the grasping. George Bernard Shaw once penned these words:

Life is no brief candle to me
It is a sort of splendid truth
That I have got hold of for the moment.

Here is your moment, your opportunity to begin creating a new legacy. Alfred Nobel, the great Swedish chemist, once opened his newspaper to read his own obituary in the local newspaper. The column read, "Alfred Nobel, the inventor of dynamite, who died yesterday, devised a way for more people to be killed in a war than ever before, and he died a very rich man."

It was Nobel's older brother who had died; a reporter got it wrong. The obituary so impacted Alfred Nobel that he made a decision to leave a very different sort of legacy. You've heard of his name, probably not for inventing dynamite, but for creating the Nobel Prize for such causes as advances in science and promotion of peace. Said Nobel, "Every man ought to have the chance to correct his epitaph in mid-stream and write a new one."

What do you want to be remembered for? If you read your obituary, what would you want said about you?

Think of those you've known and loved and depended upon who went on to the next life. Eventually, people we depend on move on. What do you recall about their lives? How did they reminisce as they came to the end?

Not long ago, a minister friend of mine told me about the pain of going through his father's severe illness. His dad was someone who'd always been there for him his whole life.

The hospital physician first told the minister the prognosis for his father—that there was nothing they could do. His heart just wouldn't hold up, and he'd die within eighteen months. It was so painful to hear these words about his father. It was even more excruciating to be the bearer of this news to his dad.

Finally, he had to tell him. They sat together in the car and through the tears, he shared with his father the doctor's prognosis about his impending death. After having the expert's pronouncements about his condition, his dad sat quietly for a few minutes and then turned to his grieving son, saying, "I know how you feel, son. It's hard. I lost my father, too."

What a perspective to carry! How amazing that, when hearing your own death sentence, you can reach out in empathy to others who are hurting. This is a vibrant, useful faith that transcends life itself.

Possess a Useful Faith

The regular prayer of my own heart is "God, don't let me be useless. Let me lead a productive, meaningful life. Let me have a vibrant faith and optimism in all I do, so my work will transcend my earthly life."

I've come to understand that without God this is impossible. It was Jesus who said, "I am the vine; you are the branches. If a man remains in me and I in him, he will bear much fruit; apart from me you can do nothing."[3]

Neither a branch nor fruit can grow on its own. It must be connected to the vine, the source of nourishment. This is true in the spiritual life as well. It is connectedness that brings about creative, meaningful existence. When Jesus said, "Apart from me you can do nothing," it didn't mean we are prevented from doing things. People can spend their whole lives involved in all sorts of tasks. Jesus was saying that, apart from a relationship with God, you can't fulfill the ultimate plan for your life. You can't find the answer for what it is in which you're truly to invest your life.

The desire to be useful is a product of our souls. It is built into the human psyche. So why do so many waste their lives and hide their talent?

Jesus once told a parable of a sower and seeds. The sower represents God, and the seed is God's word to you. Jesus said that many persons receive that seed of usefulness, purpose and meaning, but then thorns grown up around it and choke it. The thorns, Jesus explained, are primarily two things: They represent the cares of this world and the deceitfulness of riches.[4]

Those noble plans of yours can easily be choked by the world's cares—choked by time-wasters, recreation, the television, the telephone ringing, your obligations, the computer. None of these are bad in themselves at all… unless they crowd out God, and cut you off from the vine.

The deceitfulness of riches means subtly seeking after stuff that makes you feel like you've made it through the cleverness of your own plans. Living life as if you didn't need God, your ego takes over. Kenneth Blanchard once used "ego" as an acrostic, saying it could stand for Edging God Out. That's what happens. It's deceitful in that you already know this won't bring you happiness. Subtly, you've moved out further and further from the vine, until "snap," you're on your own and you begin to wither within.

Becoming this way doesn't happen overnight. A series of choices leads you down this path of uselessness to God and others. William Barclay once commented that

> God's sternest judgement is when He takes out of our
> hands the task which He meant us to do. A man has sunk
> to his lowest level when he has become useless to God.

See, what is true in physical life is often paralleled in the spiritual life. The spiritual often mirrors the natural. In this case, you use it or you lose it. For example, we know that exercising the mind over the years with reading, doing crossword puzzles and thinking helps. It keeps those synapses firing in your brain. You stay sharper. If you don't exercise your body regularly, you use it or lose it. You'll lose flexibility. You get "Dunlap's disease," where your belly "done-lapped" over your belt.

When I was a kid in elementary school, I had a defining moment once on the playground. During recess, sometimes I'd get in the center of the merry-go-round and push it, even if no one else would help me and there was a load of kids on it for a free ride.

I wasn't the biggest kid nor the smallest. For some reason, even though I was skinny, I was pretty strong—or at least determined. I remember children cheering and piling on that merry-go-round as I pushed with all my might. Round and round we went, faster and faster, and I'd hear people say, "I can't believe that Swan kid can keep going, moving all those people." I'd be in the center with my head down, gritting my teeth and thinking of a popular commercial for Twenty Mule Team Borax, which focused on the strength of the team. Even though I was alone, I'd think, "I'm just like a twenty-mule team. I can move all these people. I can push this contraption around, all by myself." And I would....

And that symbol stuck in my head—even today, as an adult. Go ahead, pile it on. I can handle it.

Really, though, on the merry-go-round of life, I discovered I can't do it myself. I need God as my co-pilot. I need God pushing beside me (and sometimes behind, pushing me!). I can do much because of the power of Jesus' words when He proclaimed,

> I tell you the truth, anyone who has faith in me will do what I have been doing. He will do even greater things than these, because I am going to the Father.[5]

With all the determination and willpower I have, I'm not capable of doing works such as Jesus did. My faith in Christ is what steers me towards a powerful, useful life.

Give Your Life Away to Others

If you are connected to God, where should your life's energies be directed, then? Jesus lived His life out to God and gave His life away to others. Following Christ's model, we see the healthiest pattern for a meaningful life.

Dr. Karl Menninger, the great dean of American psychiatry and a devout Christian man, was once asked what he would do if he found himself on the verge of a mental breakdown—about to lose it. Menninger's answer was profound. He replied, "I would close my office, go to another part of town and find someone who is in greater need than myself." Then he added, "And then I would get well."

Usefulness, altruism and fruitfulness cures you. It heals you. Helping others helps you. You feel a sense of rightness and completeness in doing what you were made to do. And no sacrifice is too large to accomplish that task.

There's a great scene in the movie *Chariots of Fire*, one of my all-time favorite motion pictures. Eric Liddell, a Christian, is training for the Olympics. It takes some juggling of schedules to train as well as continue his work as a missionary speaker. One day when his sister asks him about his tasks, he replies, "God made me fast, and when I run, I feel His pleasure." Eric Liddell was able to spread the great message in a dramatic way because of his Olympic gold medal. He helped far more people because of his fame as a runner, using that platform for Kingdom purposes.

When you do what you've supposed to be doing, you feel God's pleasure. You experience a sense of continuity in the universe. You're no longer a selfish planet of one, orbiting in your own sphere. Your life spills over into the lives of others.

Albert Schweitzer was the most admired man in the world when he passed away—one of the most beloved saints of the twentieth century. Blessed with extraordinary gifts, he could have been a world-class musician, writer, philosopher, or a professor. Early in life he was well on the way to achievements in all these fields.

Then he became captivated by the depth of human need in Africa. He went to medical school and raised money for a hospital. He gave his life away in service and in return received more honor and acclaim than one could ever expect. In losing his life, he gained it back. He wrote these words:

> You must give some time to your fellow men. Even if it's a little thing, do something for others—something for which you get no pay, but the privilege of doing it.

There's still time, with God's help, to reorient your life around Kingdom priorities. Jesus once shared a parable of a fig tree with His disciples:

> A man had a fig tree, planted in his vineyard, and he went to look for fruit on it, but did not find any. So he said to the man who took care of the vineyard, "For three years now I've been coming to look for fruit on this fig tree and haven't found any. Cut it down! Why should it use up the soil?"
> "Sir," the man replied, "leave it alone for one more year, and I'll dig around it and fertilize it. If it bears fruit next year, fine! If not, then cut it down."[6]

A fig tree normally takes three years to reach maturity. If it's not displaying fruit by then, it probably won't. In spite of that, the fig tree was given another year and another chance.

Of course, this truth is analogous to your life and mine. It tells of the God of second chances. There's still time to be useful.

Let's not fool ourselves about the brevity of time we have, though. There was a woman on the witness stand and the trial lawyer asked her, "State your age... and remember, you're under oath." She swallowed and answered, "I'm thirty-nine and some months." "How many months?" the lawyer asked. She looked away, then leaned into the microphone and said, "One hundred and eight months."

If we could only catch a glimpse of the tasks before us as seen by God! If we could but comprehend the time frame we have in which to accomplish them, it would change us.

Many of you may have seen the gripping motion picture *Schindler's List*. There's a scene at the end of the movie where the war has ended and Schindler must leave. He is surrounded by a sea of two hundred Jews whom he had been able to purchase and protect in his factory over the course of the Holocaust. Before getting into his vehicle, he looks into all the faces of the human beings he'd saved from certain death. He began to weep uncontrollably as he realizes he could have done so much more. He fingers his ring. He could have traded it for two more human lives. He looks at his car. He could have sold his car and bought ten more precious lives. He collapses in tears.

When God calls a person to make a lifetime investment, that person is called to come and die and give his or her life away. And that person will receive so much more in return.

An anonymous poem ends our thinking for the chapter:

The Dash

I read of a man who stood to speak
At the funeral of a friend
He referred to the dates on her tombstone
From the beginning to the end

He noted that first came the date of her birth
And spoke of the following date with tears
But he said what mattered most of all
Was the "dash" between those years

For that dash represents all the time
That she spent alive on earth
And now only those who loved her
Know what that little line is worth

For it matters not how much we own
The cars, the house, the cash
What matters is how we live and love
And how we spend our dash

So think about this long and hard
Are there things you'd like to change?
For you never know how much time is left
(You could be at "dash mid-range")

If we could just slow down enough
To consider what's true and real
And always try to understand
Like we've never loved before

If we treat each other with respect
And more often wear a smile
Remembering that this special dash
Might only last a little while

So when your eulogy's being read
With your life's actions to rehash
Would you be proud of the things they say
About how you spent your dash?

A man's steps are directed by the Lord.
How then can anyone understand his own way?

—PROVERBS 20:24, NIV

Young men are apt to think themselves wise enough, as drunken men are
apt to think themselves sober enough.

—LORD CHESTERFIELD

Nature gives man corn, but he must grind it. God gives me a will, but
he must make the right choices.

—BISHOP FULTON SHEEN

There is a way that seems right *to a man but in the end it leads to death.*
—PROVERBS 16:25, NIV; AUTHOR'S EMPHASIS

If only one could have two lives. The first in which to make one's mis-
takes and the second in which to profit by them.

—D.H. LAWRENCE

Life is what happens to you when you're busy making other plans.

—JOHN LENNON

For this God is our God for ever and ever;
he will be our guide even to the end.

—PSALM 48:14, NIV

You have made known to me the path of life.

—PSALM 16:11, NIV

Chief Justice Oliver Wendell Holmes once lost his ticket after boarding
a train in Washington, D.C. The conductor recognized him and said
not to worry. The ticket could be mailed in when found. Justice Holmes
replied, "But Mr. Conductor, my question is not 'where is my ticket?' but
'where am I supposed to be going?'"

Can I Know God's Will?

"Directions, please!"

*N*early everyone I know has a pet peeve that irritates them at some level. It may be people who patronize, or persons who let their dogs run loose, or individuals who take what is obviously thirty items or more into the grocery express lane clearly marked "Ten items or less" or guys who channel-surf constantly.

I've got a pet peeve. I wish it didn't bother me, but it does. It's when other drivers don't use turn signals. A driver suddenly stops in the lane in front of you without any acknowledgment of where the car is going… and eventually turns left. Or you're at a stoplight which has just turned green, waiting to turn left, and your left signal is blinking. The car across the light from you doesn't use a signal and you have to sit and wait trying to figure out what he will do. Finally, without ever displaying direction, he turns left directly in front of you.

It's a small thing, I know. And with many such instances like that, it got me thinking about a connection with turn signals and the spiritual life. The New Testament alone uses eighteen Greek words for the word we translate as "turn" in English. It's an important word.

It generally means going one direction and then going another. The word "conversion" comes from the same root. It can mean to twist from the base. While driving, many people don't use turn signals because *they don't think before they turn.* The spiritual analogy is putting little thought into turning towards big decisions—making impulse choices. Buy this car, this house, and this one-time offer. Before you know it, you've turned a big corner and are headed down a road called debt.

The same is true about deeply emotional decisions such as marriage or dating relationships. These are huge choices in your life. Look at the mess so many people have made of their lives as a result of their ill-planned judgements.

Another reason many people don't use turn signals is *they don't really care about other drivers.* A selfish orientation—just watch out for one's own self on the road of life. Get out of my way!

Jesus once told a story about people who ignored a needy man on a road and a Good Samaritan who watched out for others on the road and was helpful and courteous. A spiritual person is an unselfish person, for this reflects the very heart of God who even gave up His own Son to die on our behalf.

A final and most common reason I believe many people don't use turn signals is *they don't know where they're going.* You've been behind such drivers before. They look around, rubbernecking, eyes everywhere except on the road, just cruising through life: speed up, slow down, brakes on, brakes off—no rhythm whatsoever.

In the spiritual realm, I really believe people are lost without God through Jesus Christ. Jesus Himself once called people "blind guides." He said to Nicodemus, "Except a man be born again, he cannot see the kingdom of God."[1]

Jesus explained, "Except you *turn* and be converted you shall not see the kingdom of God." God signals a person, via the Holy Spirit, to turn towards a way that leads to peace, purpose and everlasting life.

Living without Christ is like driving a car with the front end out of alignment. You can stay on the road if you grip the steering wheel with both hands and hold tightly. A lapse of attention, however, and you head straight for the ditch and a crash. It is a ceaseless struggle. Coming to God is like getting a front-end alignment for your life. God does an inner work in you from the base and gives you a moral compass so you can stay on the right road.

You've no doubt made some wrong turns in your life. You may be a very competent person in many ways. You might be able to repair a machine or run a computer or play a sport well, but have no idea how to navigate your inner life.

Not to worry. God *does* have a plan for your life. The prophet Jeremiah once spoke comforting words of direction.

> "For I know the plans I have for you," declares the Lord, "plans to prosper you and not to harm you, plans to give you hope and a future. Then you will call upon me and come and pray to me, and I will listen to you. You will seek me and find me when you seek me with all your heart." (Jeremiah 29:11–14).

Sincere truth-seekers will always ask, "What does God want for my life?" I call this big monster question that looms over our lives "Godswilla" (say it out loud once or twice). There is no need to be afraid of God's will. The apostle Paul describes God's will as "good, perfect and pleasing."[2]

God promises to guide us.

> I will instruct you and teach you in the way you should go; I will counsel you and watch over you.
> Do not be like the horse or the mule,
> which have no understanding
> but must be controlled by bit and bridle

or they will not come to you.
Many are the woes of the wicked,
but the LORD's unfailing love
surrounds the man who trusts in him (Psalm 32:8–10).

God wants to give you a good life laden with peace, meaning and hope. Too many of us are like the stubborn mule the psalmist refers to in the aforementioned Scripture passage. We really believe we know what's right for our lives and that God's will is an intrusion on our happy plans. It is an enormously inaccurate picture of God's plan.

Paul Little sums up this erroneous belief in *Affirming the Will of God*:

> We have the tragic, mistaken idea that we must choose between doing what we want to do and being happy, and doing what God wants us to do and being miserable. We think the will of God is some horrible thing which he sort of shoves under our nose and demands, "All right, are you willing, are you willing?" If we could just get out from under his clammy hands we could really swing.
>
> Nothing could be further from the truth. Such notions are a slur on the character of God. So many of us see God as a kind of celestial Scrooge who peers over the balcony of heaven trying to find anybody who is enjoying life. And when he spots a really happy person, he yells, "Now cut that out." That concept of God should make us shudder because it's blasphemous.[3]

Understand that the God of the universe loves you and wants to fill your life with His beautiful will. But *you* have to want it as well.

Commitment

How do we begin to step into God's will? It's a decision, really. Like every journey of a thousand miles, it starts with a single step. You must decide you want to do it more than performing any of your personal plans and schemes. A psalmist wrote that

> Better is one day in your courts than a thousand elsewhere:
> I would rather be a doorkeeper in the house of my God
> than dwell in the tents of the wicked.[4]

Russ Johnston, in his book *How to Know the Will of God*, comments:

> God does not reveal His will to curiosity seekers. If you are thinking, "God, if You let me know Your will, I'll decide if I can do it." God will not allow you to see it. He doesn't work that way. Jesus outlined God's plan this way: "If a man chooses to do God's will, he will find out whether my teaching comes from God or whether I speak on my own" (John 7:17). What Jesus is saying is that if you are willing to do, then you will know. This is something the whole of scripture teaches: if you were to stack up all the verses in the Bible on doing the will of God in one place, and all the verses in the Bible on knowing the will of God in another, there would be a giant pile on doing and a skinny and little stack on knowing. Because once you've committed to do, knowing comes easy.[5]

This is an important point. There's a never-ending discussion over whether doing for God is more significant than being in God. It's a moot issue to me. Both are important. Doing God's will leads you closer to being in God's presence. Being in God's presence leads to being filled with a desire to do all things for God. Right living leads to right attitudes. Right attitude leads to righteous living. Both bring about character development, for ultimately who you are is infinitely more significant than anything you do. D.L. Moody once claimed that character is who you are in the dark. It's the private victories, the quiet moments alone, the resisting of temptations that shape a character acceptable and pleasing to God.

As you offer yourself to God, sacrificing, giving and learning, your mind becomes transformed. As a result, you start to think "God-thoughts," and you're able to better discern God's will. [6]

Calling

You have a call from God on your life. It's a call in which the journey itself is as important as the destination. The Book of Numbers describes how the people of Israel were led to the Promised Land by a cloud during the day and a pillar of fire at night. When it moved, they moved; when it stayed, they stayed. Never in history has there ever been a more direct guidance to a people, and yet we refer to it as "wandering in the wilderness" for forty years.

Never call it that again. God was purifying, testing, changing even as He was taking them to a destination. So it is in our lives. It may seem like we're in a wilderness for a long time, when in fact the journey was needed so we'd be in a place of total receptivity to God's will.

This path, this pilgrimage takes two forms. There is a general call and a specific call. The general call is to accept Jesus Christ as Savior and Lord and live for God. The apostle Peter wrote, "To this you were called, because Christ suffered for you, leaving you an example, that you should follow in his steps."[7] This is the general call for all persons.

Those who have not chosen to follow Jesus Christ simply play at the game of life. They may believe they're involved in the game, but the truth is they're not even in the batter's box yet. Jesus spoke of a broad path that leads to destruction and many are on it. There's lots of company. There is also a narrow path that few find, and it leads to eternal life. It's well worn for you—simply follow the footsteps of Jesus Christ.

Not only is there a general call, there is a specific call. John Calvin wrote that

> There is a universal call by which God… invites all men alike. Here is a specific call which for the most part God bestows on believers only.

I think of it like having a Christian business card, a "calling card." If you had a Christian calling card "to be about the Lord's business," what would it say? It would, of course, have your title— what you specifically do and uniquely contribute to God's work here on earth.

Your unique talents and gifts were given to you to be used for God and others. Paul wrote, "for God's gifts and his call are irrevocable."[8] Irrevocable means you can't go back on it. Once you cross that line, once you commit your life to follow Christ, you have stepped into your destiny. Your specific talents come to full function. You are God's son or daughter, with an inheritance and a special calling.

Choices

Shortly before actor Peter Sellers' death, his fourth wife, actress Lynne Fredrick, shared this about her husband: "His mind is in a constant turmoil about his purpose on this planet and whether it's all worthwhile."

No person should have to live with such a confused manner. Daily, you should be able to discern the most worthwhile purposes and plans for your life. Perhaps when you were a child, you heard the phrase, "stop, look and listen." While this applied to crossing a street, it can also apply to the choices made at regular crossroads in your spiritual journey. You can stop, look and listen for one or more of several directions that will lead you closer to ascertaining God's will.

The prophet Jeremiah encouraged us to "Set up road signs; put up guideposts. Take note of the highway, the road that you take."[9]

Scripture is the primary means by which we ascertain God's will. God's will is never in contradiction with His Word. Most of God's will is already revealed in the Bible. The great majority of your decisions will be tempered by the simple question, "What do the Scriptures say in this case?" The psalmist wrote, "Your statutes are my delight; they are my counselors."[10] The Bible becomes a kind of objective guidebook, freeing you from having to make God's will a greatly subjective, ambiguous issue.

The still small voice or *gentle impressions* are another means for laying hold of God's will. This is more subjective area where we can easily substitute our inner thoughts and desires for God's voice.

It's a learning curve. A wise business executive was asked why he was so successful. His answer: right decisions. He was then asked how he learned to make right decisions. His answer: wrong decisions.

Sometimes, perhaps often, we'll err in discerning the small voice behind us that Isaiah the prophet said would guide us. When my son was four years old, he told me he was hearing voices speak to him. Naturally interested, I asked what the voices said to him. He replied that whenever he was thinking of doing something wrong, the voice would say, "No, no, no—don't you do that." Then he looked up at me quizzically and asked, "Is that the voice of God?"

I don't know for sure if it was God. It might have been the past voices of his parents in his head. The principle is the same, though. There is a still, small voice that can guide us. When God spoke to the prophet Elijah, it was a gentle whisper.[11] Jesus said that His sheep would know His voice.[12] Over time you begin to distinguish the voice of God from the other sounds clamoring for your attention.

I have blown countless small decisions in my life, but I have confidence that, with God's grace, I've been relatively successful on making the large decisions according to His will—big choices like that of a marriage partner, where to go to college and where to work were all preceded by times of quietness and seeking to "tune in" to the Holy Spirit. Perhaps because of my almost desperate fear of missing God's will, I sought to calm my soul so I could hear the gentle whisper of God's voice and have deep abiding peace about my decision.

The apostle Paul wrote about having the peace of Christ ruling in our hearts.[13] The word "rule" can be translated "umpire." Umpires make the final call or decision in sporting events. When you are in the throes of a decision and seeking God's will, the peace of God can be the umpire in helping you to make the right call. God's gentle voice may on occasion be urgent, but generally it is loving, quiet and peaceable. When you "pray through" and receive a "peace that passes all understanding," God is reassuring and guiding you.

Common sense is a third area of guidance. God has given you a mind. You have the Spirit of God within you. With the spirit of reason, you can make many decisions that do not require deep impressions or special insights.

For example, I am a husband and father. My wife and I are parents to two remarkable children who are now young adults. While they were small, I came to realize that some of my vocational obligations were keeping me from the time needed to nurture and impact them during the short period of their lives they would be at home. Common sense dictated that a big part of my life's calling was to give much time, attention and energy towards the lives of these beautiful human beings. I made some big lifestyle changes in order to give attention to their needs.

You may have known persons who are so heavenly minded that they're no earthly good. This is an anomaly, an irregularity. The devout Christian should be the most useful and productive of persons on the earth.

The sensibility of the Holy Spirit is the most uncommon common sense of all. It dwells in its fullness in every Christian, teaching how to walk in God's will.

Visions and dreams are yet another means of discerning God's will. There are many examples in the Bible of persons to whom God gave direction in a vision or a dream. Joseph was a dreamer. Paul was given a total new direction after his vision. Jacob's dream changed him forever. Peter's vision led him to embrace the rest of the world beyond Judaism.

Pay attention to your dreams. Much of the time, dreams may be no more than conflicts you're still working out or the result of too much pepperoni pizza. Sometimes, though, when your shield is down while asleep, the Holy Spirit may be delivering a symbolic message. Be cognizant of your visions as well. We don't have to over-spiritualize this. God may put a desire in your heart to do or be something. It may come early in life.

When I was seven years of age, my precious mother recorded in her diary my expressed desire to become a minister some day. It was my early calling from God. It was a dream put in my heart.

In my teens, I was attracted to the work of a high-school guidance counselor. I saw first-hand the value of personal counseling and guidance in an educational setting. I felt I had the personal gifts to be effective in this area of counseling psychology as well.

Contradictory calls? Opposing dreams and visions? Not at all. Today I serve God as a professor of psychology and religion; I'm a minister who teaches and counsels at a terrific college.

This leads to a fifth area of guidance. *Wise counsel* can be a critical, buffering means of discerning God's will. The writer of Proverbs penned that "in the multitude of counsellors there is safety."[14] Solomon knew this fact as a wise king. He wrote, "Plans fail for lack of counsel, but with advisors they succeed" (Proverbs 15:22).

Wise persons seek guidance from trusted, faithful, mature men and women. When I was eighteen and a college freshman, I was deeply dissatisfied with where I was going. Even though I'd done well scholastically in high school, my first-year college grades were mediocre. I was majoring in friends, fun and Friday nights. I was a good American—I believed in the two-party system: a party Friday night and a party Saturday night. However, I'd look in the mirror on Sunday morning and I didn't like what I was becoming. I was just meandering through life.

Most of you readers have been in such a place. Perhaps you're there right now. A night of alcohol or drugs mixed with levity and shallow relationships can't mask inner emotional pain. A big smile and false bravado won't fool anyone. Fortunately, I was blessed to have wise people in my life whom I could seek out and bounce off ideas for some radical changes in my life. Over the next several months I followed through, and I've never been the same since.

Finally, *circumstances* can help you appropriate the direction of God's will. In Ephesians, chapter five, believers are told to walk circumspectly, looking carefully around in a circle. Actually, some would suggest that, for people walking closely with God, there are no circumstances, only divine appointments.

Be aware of doors and opportunities that come about in your life. Note the people brought into your path. God doesn't shine the light of His will for you far into the future, but just a step at a time. The psalmist said God was a lamp unto his feet and a light unto his path.[15] The will of God may well be directly in front of you. It is a sense of timeliness.

The Book of Esther tells a wonderful story of a Jewess promoted to a queen just as her people were about to be exterminated. Her father, Mordecai, noted to Esther "And who knows but that you have come to royal position for such a time as this?"[16] Indeed she was, and the thrilling story displays how God can work mightily in the midst of the most dire of circumstances.

You were born for this time. Look around and see how you might be utilized. One young missionary was asked when she received her call to the mission field. She replied it came with her conversion to Christ. Doesn't that make sense? The need was so great, and she simply responded.

As I was in my final months of a three-year Army obligation, I was in enormous conflict over where to go to college. I was in Louisiana at the time. My plans evolved around moving back home to the state of Wisconsin and attending school within nearby range of family. I prayed night and day about what to do, since I knew the choice of school would dramatically impact my whole life.

An opportunity to attend a John Denver concert in a nearby city gave me a chance to visit a college campus there. That simple choice led to a full scholarship, a change in denominational direction, a new major, a wonderful wife and a fine education. Be aware of the "circumstances" that surround you right now.

In all these six means of determining the will of God, there is interdependence between you and the sovereignty of God. It's like being on a sailboat which has a predetermined destination, but while on board, all the crew and passengers have freedom to move about as they please. Your life is propelled toward a destiny by the breeze of the Holy Spirit, yet you can guide the rudder to coincide with it or against it, towards it or away from it. Decide for it and live in the center of God's will.

If the Lord delights in a man's way,
he makes his steps firm;
though he stumble, he will not fall,
for the Lord upholds him with his hand.

—PSALM 37: 23–24, NIV

Always walk into a place like you belong—and most people believe
you do.

—ED MCMAHON

It is the state of our wills that establishes the state of our lives.

—WILLIAM LAW

Many of us spend half our time wishing for things we could have if we
didn't spend half our time wishing.

—ALEXANDER WOOLLCOTT

Two paths diverged upon a wood and I took the one less traveled by, and
that has made all the difference.

—ROBERT FROST

The world stands aside to let anyone pass who knows where he is going.

—DAVID STARR JORDAN

Every tomorrow has two handles. We can take hold of it with the handle
of anxiety or the handle of faith.

—HENRY WARD BEECHER

Destiny is not a matter of chance; it is a matter of choice.
It is not a thing to be wanted for; it is a thing to be achieved.

—WILLIAM JENNINGS BRYAN

How Can I Get the Big Decisions Right?

"Be careful that you're not too careful!"

The Christian life is meant to be a calculated risk, not a blind faith. Because of the person, message, and especially the resurrection of Jesus Christ from the dead, people are called to step out of the deadness of a meager existence and embrace life.

The truth is, most people—even Christians—live a life of what could be called "functional atheism." They believe in their minds that there is a God, but there is little demonstration of that fact in how they make everyday decisions.

For people who are serious about following God, there are always decisions and risks involved. You see it in the lives of biblical characters.

Abraham had to leave his homeland.

Moses had to lead the people of Israel out of Egypt to the Promised Land.

Peter immediately left his fishing nets to follow Jesus.

Each was taking a risk. A risk of faith. A calculated risk, because it was based on the premise that "If this was God's direction for me, then God will take care of me." Most individuals lack this perspective.

They are lacking the adventurous spirit characterized by the biblical heroes. Wes Seeliger once called it a "settler spirit" versus a "pioneer spirit." A settler spirit stays put. A pioneer spirit has an open optimism towards what life may bring his or her way.

I notice the older I get, the more careful I become. And I don't want to be too careful or too guarded. Someone has said the only exercise some people get is exercising caution. There's a saying used at the college where I work that fits here: "If you keep doing what you're doing, you'll just keep getting what you're getting." Same old, same old.

I once read about the African impala, an incredible leaping animal capable of jumping to a height of ten feet and a distance of thirty feet. Yet, a zoo can contain these animals with a simple three-foot retaining wall. The reason? An impala won't jump if he's unable to see where his feet will fall!

Part of the excitement (and no little trepidation) of Christian life is not knowing where your feet will fall. It causes a person to seek faith. The apostle Paul once wrote, "So then faith cometh by hearing, and hearing by the word of God" (Romans 10:17, KJV). This underscores the importance of reading the Bible for not only direction in life, but also for the faith to act upon it. The Bible is often referred to as "God's Word," because God speaks to you through these pages. And if you listen, God is speaking about living more by faith.

In some ways we're all like the woman who woke up one morning unable to speak, suffering from severe laryngitis. To help her communicate, her husband developed a system of "taps" that represented various words and phrases. One tap stood for "Yes." Two taps meant "No." Ninety-three taps meant "take out the garbage."

Some of you reading may need ninety-three taps on the shoulder before you can truly recognize the voice of God. However, there comes a time where thinking and listening isn't enough. Faith is meant to be put into action. There comes a time when you leave the settler spirit behind.

Break Away From the Pack

As a young adult, I made a decision to be a pioneer—to break away from the pack. Up to that point, I was much more of a sheep than I like to admit.

At age eighteen, I made a list of goals for myself that I wanted to reach by age thirty. At that time, thirty years of age seemed to be forever and a day away. I laid my list aside and forgot about it... or so it seemed. Fifteen years later, on a visit to my parents' house, my mother gave me a box of various items from my childhood and adolescence. I sorted through them all, making a trip down memory lane. Then I came to a yellowed sheet of paper listing the goals I wanted to reach at age thirty. Amazingly, I had reached all these goals, for they had unconsciously guided me on my life's journey.

I realized I had made the transformation from settler to pioneer. I had made the critical choices that propelled me to success. I had pulled away from the pack. I had resisted conforming to what nearly everyone else in my very small universe was doing.

This bent to group conformity is a hard thing to resist. Americans, especially, like to think of themselves as rugged individualists. The truth is, we're a lot like sheep. We follow the crowd much more than we like to admit.

I was reminded of this when a large group of sixty or seventy motorcyclists drove into our city and parked themselves for a mid-evening break at a central shopping center parking lot. I was slowly driving by in backed-up traffic and was able to observe these bikers. I was sure that any of them would have described himself or herself as a real individual. No bowing to society. Hell-raisers, every one—or at least, that's what some of the tee-shirts proclaimed.

On second look, however, I realized they were all essentially dressed alike. It was like a uniform of sorts. Think of bikers' dress. Tight jeans, black tee-shirts, boots, leather jackets, tattoos, red bandannas, facial hair (even the women—it was gross). And they all drove the same brand of bike: Harleys.

No deviation here. No real individualism. Follow the pack and practice pack behavior. Conformists, every one.

A key point in maturation is when you not only realize that you've been a nearly pure conformist, you decide to do something about it. It's like reaching a crossroads. Actually, throughout adulthood, we pass through a number of crossroads moments where we have distinctive choices to make. And the choices made shape us in very significant ways.

It's been written that everyone is born an original and dies a copy. The great realization that came to me in early adulthood was that it was the closest opportunity I might ever have to start over.

I do a lot of speaking to high school and college students. I tell them that once you enter the adult world and leave the artificial atmosphere of high school, you start over. Nobody in the adult world cares whether you were the homecoming queen or captain of an athletic team or in the "in-clique" or a big deal in high school. Whether you were quiet, shy, unpopular or in the "out group" is equally of no consequence. The rules change. It's almost like a blank slate. It can be liberating. A little scary, but liberating. *You* get to decide to move out from the pack or not.

Choices

So, what kind of choices will you make? It was Plato who developed the argument that you cannot know the one without having considered the many. That is, one cannot choose the best without having considered all the choices.

In Christianity, there is one big choice that must be made in order to pull the other decisions into proper alignment. The starting place for all our choices begins with an eternal decision. This decision was framed in a few words by Joshua to the people of Israel shortly before his death, when he said, "Choose for yourselves this day whom you will serve…"

Here is where we begin. Choose God or false gods. Serve a Savior or serve yourself. Worship your Creator or worship the creation. The Living Bible's translation of Job's words in chapter thirty-four put it well:

> We can choose the sounds we want to listen to; we can choose the taste we want in food; and we should choose to follow what is right; but first of all, we must define among ourselves what is good.

In defining goodness, we choose to embrace the source of all that is good: a God that is not only good, but merciful, gracious, kind, compassionate and patient. A God we would want to serve. A God who can be trusted for guidance in the big decisions in life.

In the military, a distinction is made between strategy and tactics. Strategy, of course, is the overall plan. Tactics make up the carrying out of hundreds of pieces of that plan. A soldier can be forgiven for mistakes in tactics, but little leeway is given to the soldier who errs in his strategic plan. What is true in military planning is most certainly true for life planning. A correct life strategy is essential to success. Errors in the tactical carrying out of that plan will occur often. It certainly has in my case. Tactical errors will be forgiven; an incorrect strategy will not.

For people of the Christian faith, the strategy starts with choosing to serve God. You'll serve someone or something all your life; why not let it be the Creator of the universe?

Vocation

Two huge decisions present themselves early in adulthood. One is *vocation*: what am I going to spend my life doing? The word *vocation* is derived from Latin and refers to being called. Called to a particular task while alive on planet earth.

What you do as an occupation is of no little significance. Each of us has a necessary place. And we can come to that decision by considering various factors:

Enjoyment—do you enjoy a certain kind of work? Do you feel a passionate interest in a particular field? God forbid that you would spend your entire life in a career just because it paid well, or gave you a nice pension in the end or because your parents did this sort of work.

Aptitude—do you have a special ability or affinity for this occupation? Do your studies reflect higher scores? On career or personality assessments, do you do well in the areas that generally lead to success in this field?

Earnings—can you make a living and support a family with this work? Perhaps you would have to be a "starving artist" or "pay your dues" for a while until financial reward comes your way.

Requirements—do you need certain training for this work? For example, you would need to go to nursing school to become an R.N., but are you able to get in?

God's will—if you have the supernatural peace and assurance God wants this for your life, then no human obstacle can forever prevent you from achieving it. Where there is a will (God's will), there is a way.

An important thought about these various factors—you need to get them all right in order to work. That's why this enormous decision should be a great matter of thought, investigation and prayer in order to get it right.

Marriage

Marriage is the other huge decision we make in life. Some will choose not to marry. Most, however, will be faced with a decision that can bring either great meaning or great harm to their lives.

Socrates encouraged marriage. "By all means, marry," he said. "If you get a good wife, you will become very happy; if you get a bad one, you will become a philosopher and that is good for every man."

People are hesitant to marry at this point in history. Fractured families litter the American landscape. We've all been impacted at some emotional level by the amount of pain resulting from poor marriages. Naturally, such a level of concern would cause us to seek for divine answers.

You may have heard of the woman who was walking down the street one day when she heard a voice call out, "Stop! If you take another step, you'll be killed." She stopped and a second later, an errant brick fell from a building right in her path.

Later that day, the woman was about to cross the street when she heard the same voice yell, "Stop! Don't cross the street." As she hesitated for a second, a delivery truck came barreling around the corner without stopping for the red light.

Shaken, the woman sat down. She asked loudly, "Who are you?" A ghostly voice replied, "I'm your guardian angel. I bet you have some questions for me."

"I sure do," the woman said. "Where were you on my wedding day?"

Seriously, the question of choosing the right marriage partner is an enormous issue. You may wonder, though, whether God has already picked out a partner for you.

While conscientious Christians line up on both sides of this question, I am one who believes God calls us into marriage with a specific person. I am comforted by the fact that God prepared Eve for Adam. In fact, when Adam meets Eve the first time, in essence he says, "This is it!"

Adam was really saying, "This is her. This was Your intention for me, God. A committed lifelong relationship with another human being. Love, honor—and oh, boy!"

While single individuals, my wife and I prayed that God would lead us to the right person. We've learned you can't pick the person, time or place, but God will answer that prayer of your heart. Because of this, I've prayed for my children's spouses for many years now. My children are both single young adults at the time of this writing. I know that somewhere out there is a wife for my son and a husband for my daughter. I have prayer daily for these two individuals I've not yet met. Someday, though, each will bring a fiancé home and I'll see these persons for whom I've been praying for such a long time.

What kinds of factors enter into this decision?

A shared faith—this is at the top of my list. The Bible warns against being unequally yoked (2 Corinthians 6:14). Are you praying about marrying a person who doesn't believe in God? Don't waste your breath. It's quite clear that light and darkness can't have fellowship. There is no such thing, generally, as missionary dating where you date a person to bring him or her to faith. This may seem harsh to some readers, but I didn't create the rules. After all, if God is the center and source of meaning in your life, how could you be deeply intimate with another person who doesn't understand this at all?

Flexibility ranks highly in the personality attribute department. A couple will weather many changes together over a lifetime. That's why it's important to date a person a long time, usually at least a year, to see how that person reacts to the nuances and contours of a changing, adapting relationship.

Loyalty is a must. Think about it. What if you married someone who was attractive, witty, charming and a good provider, but wasn't loyal to you, rather, unfaithful. Unfaithfulness tends to negate nearly every positive attribute a person can display.

Marry someone who will be loyal, someone who will keep his or her commitments. I remember Fred Smith relaying a story about being in a restaurant seated next to a table in which a young couple sat together. After the couple finished their dessert, he got up, paid for the bill and walked out. It seemed like odd behavior.

Then, a minute later, the young husband returned to his wife and she stretched out her arms toward him as he picked her up. The wife was wearing a full body brace. Her husband gently carried her out of the restaurant and carefully put her through the open door of his pickup truck into the seat.

Everyone in the restaurant had stopped to watch, and it became very quiet in there until a waitress finally spoke the words on everybody's mind: "My, he sure took his vows seriously."

Compatibility is also critical. Do you share common interests? Similar humor? Do your life goals mesh to some degree? You don't have to be totally compatible. You never will be, and that's part of the learning experience of marriage. To a degree, you will learn to be more compatible over the years living with the same person.

Altruism—this word may not show up on a lot of lists. Altruism has to do with other-centeredness. It is the opposite of selfishness. God forbid that you would marry a very selfish person.

Does she or he show interest in your projects and ask you questions… and actually listen? Is he or she a helpful individual?

Marriage involves a lot of giving. Altruistic individuals already have a disposition that will put them miles ahead in this department.

Kindness—a minister-mentor of mine always asked about this early in premarital counseling. Observe this person carefully and see if he or she treats others kindly. Is she or he patient? Even take a good look at how this person treats animals.

One of the time-honored rituals of serious dating is when the family invites you over for a meal with them. Their intent is to look you over as a potential son- or daughter-in-law. Don't shy away from this opportunity. Scrutinize them as well. Especially watch how your intended treats his/her family. If family members are treated with great kindness and patience, chances are the same treatment will be yours when you become family. On the other hand, if family members are met with indifference or unkindness, when you become family you may get the same treatment.

Marriage is a deeply spiritual decision. It also involves a lot of common sense. Use your head as well as following your heart while guided by your soul. This is good advice for any big decision.

If you don't find satisfaction in this world, you're maybe made for another.

—C.S. LEWIS

Delight yourself in the Lord and He will give you the desires of your heart.

—PSALM 37:4, NKJV

The only way to avoid being miserable is to not have enough leisure to wonder whether you're happy or not.

—GEORGE BERNARD SHAW

Contentment is natural wealth; luxury, artificial poverty.

—SOCRATES

But godliness with contentment is great gain. For we brought nothing into the world and we can take nothing out of it. But if we have food and clothing, we will be content with that.

—1 TIMOTHY 6:6–8, KJV

I don't know what your destiny will be, but one thing I know: the only ones among you who will really be happy are those who have sought and found how to serve.

—ALBERT SCHWEITZER

To be of use in this world is the only way to be happy.

—HANS CHRISTIAN ANDERSON

It's not your position in life that will make you happy; it's your disposition.

—UNKNOWN

Nevertheless, each one should retain the place in life that the Lord assigned to him and to which God has called him.

—1 CORINTHIANS 7:17, NIV

To get what you want, give others what they need.

—MICHAEL BRYANT

Can I Find Satisfaction in This Life?

"Life, liberty, and the pursuit of happiness?"

A popular magazine polled influential people in the music business and asked them to rate the best rock-and-roll songs in the first half-century of rock's existence (1950–2000). The choice: *I Can't Get No Satisfaction* by the Rolling Stones.

What an apt title and appropriate choice. For as much excitement and titillation rock music—or any music, for that matter—may bring into one's life, it never truly satisfies.

Satisfaction is a nebulous term. It refers to being made happy, which is even more elusive. Happiness comes from the old English word "hap," or "happenstance," which refers to chance. Therefore, satisfaction is a chancy thing. And Americans, despite all their economic and social progress, are less satisfied than ever before.

The Facts

F. Scott Fitzgerald once referred to our "thinning briefcases of enthusiasm." Despite having much more, we are enjoying it much less. From almost any angle, the last century has been a dream for the United States.

Comparing the one-hundred-year span to now, we see:

Academic Success—at the turn of the century, only thirteen percent of the adult population had high-school diplomas. Today, the figure is eighty-three percent.

Health Accomplishments—in 1900, an adult could expect to live to be forty-seven years old. Today the average is seventy-seven years of longevity.

Conveniences—most Americans didn't have electricity, flush toilets or central heating one hundred years ago; now, they are common expectations for all.

Income—adjusted to twenty-first century dollars, the average working citizen makes over three times what a worker made in the first decade of the twentieth century.

And yet, if we have it so good, why do we perceive that it's so bad? The homicide rate went up almost five-fold in a century, divorce is rampant, school shootings are weekly news and the American crime rate rivals or significantly exceeds that of any of the nations of the world to whom we compare ourselves.[1]

The facts are that income, convenience, health and education don't necessarily spell satisfaction.

A man once complained to Benjamin Franklin about the happiness the Constitution was supposed to guarantee. Franklin's wise reply: "The Constitution doesn't guarantee happiness; just the pursuit of it. You have to catch it yourself."

The facts are that we're not happy on our own. Not that it's a new problem. Cynicism and disillusionment have always been with us. Read these words:

The earth is degenerating these days. Bribery and corruption abound. Children no longer mind parents. Every man wants to write a book and it is evident that the end of the world is approaching fast.

These words could have been written in today's newspaper editorial. Actually, they were found inscribed on a five-thousand-year-old Assyrian stone tablet.

Look at this statement a senator made to his peers:

I fear for our nation. Nearly half of our people receive some form of government subsidy. We have grown weak from too much affluence and too little adversity. I fear that soon we will not be able to defend our country from sure and certain enemies. We have debased our currency to the point that even the most loyal citizen no longer trusts it.

Sound familiar? Those words *were* spoken by a senator. A *Roman* senator, in A.D. sixty-three. They could have been spoken by a U.S. senator today. Dissatisfaction has always been a malaise of advanced societies.

The Illusion

If those are the facts, then the continued illusion is that we can somehow be satisfied on our own. While driving and vacationing in Canada, I saw two contradictory advertisements. One advertisement had the slogan "*Obey* Your Thirst." Another ad promoted the idea, "*Check* Your Thirst." To which one should we give in? Do we give in to all our natural drives and desires, or are we called to check and channel our powerful drives?

In the twenty-first-century American culture, the continual drumbeat is to follow your compulsions and give expression to whatever you're feeling—unless, of course, the practice is currently politically incorrect or out of fashion.

To a degree, all of us are driven by our needs. These deep-seated, often subconscious drives compel us towards all sorts of directions. If you want to understand yourself, it's helpful to categorize some of the basic drives.

The most basic drive would concern *survival* issues. Much of people's behavior can be explained by the primary need for food, air and shelter. However, if these primary needs are met, there is another step up the ladder. These could be called *comfort* needs.

Freud referred to the pleasure principle. If a behavior brings us pleasure and is not immediately life-threatening, chances increase that we will repeat the behavior. Think of activities people participate in that bring pleasure but might hurt them in the long run: overeating, smoking and alcohol/drug indulgence are a few that come to mind.

Security would be another drive that manifests when one's survival and comfort needs are met. It seems to be a function of insuring that the primary things in life one has gotten used to will always be there. We don't just want it now; we want it for the future as well. In a society such as the United States that helps supply the primary needs, security has risen to the forefront of concern. From Social Security to job security, to pensions to insurance, Americans are obsessed with this issue.

Beyond survival, comfort and security, there is yet one greater need and it is the issue of this chapter. *Satisfaction*. A good paycheck is not enough; job satisfaction is equally or more important. A decent marriage is not enough; a couple wants a healthy, satisfying relationship.

Satisfaction appears to be a central life-urge along with the twin feelings of peace and contentment.[2] So, check your thirst or obey your thirst? The writer of Proverbs suggests that you will never be satisfied if you simply obey your thirsts: "Hell and destruction are never full, so the eyes of man are never satisfied."[3]

The Apostle John in his first epistle called it:

- *the lust of the flesh*
- *the lust of the eyes*
- *the pride of life.*

All of these are from the world rather than from God.[4]

This is Satan's great trick. This is the great illusion. People think they'll be satisfied by these things and they aren't.

R.C. Sproul has said that the problem with giving your life to pleasure, defining what is good as what is pleasurable, is that you'll experience the hedonistic paradox. The hedonist paradox or dilemma is this:

- If you can't get the pleasure you want, you'll be frustrated.

- If you do get the pleasure you want, eventually you'll become bored with it.

Either way, you lose.

The *lust of the flesh* is an insatiable appetite. I've lost track of the number of people I've counseled over the years who thought an affair would make them happy and instead it devastated their world. The persuasive influence of pornography has escalated dramatically, with millions of men addicted to sex in magazines, on the Internet, television or the telephone. Or that Satan would pull the ultimate deception—to convince a person that his or her body was made for the same gender. The lust of the flesh never ends.

The *lust of the eyes* refers to covetousness. Always wanting more—always keeping up with the proverbial Joneses! My wife and I are at a stage in our lives where we have obtained many of the props and possessions for which most people hunger and strive all life long. And yet we realize these items have made us no happier than we were in our first two years of marriage, living in a fourteen-by-thirty-two-foot apartment in graduate housing. We had little in the way of material things and were as happy as could be. We married for each other, not for what we had or didn't have.

I think of the newly married man who asked his wife, "Darling, would you have married me if my father hadn't left me a fortune?" His wife sweetly replied, "Honey, I would have married you no matter *who* left you the fortune." Think about it.

The *pride of life* is so subtle. We can be so proud of our titles or our degrees. Actually, anything can slip over into this category.

A few years ago, I received some seed grant money and embarked on a second doctoral program. I already have five degrees, and after a residency year of study, came to my senses. What did I need two doctorates for? Would I be called "Doctor, Doctor"? It was the pride of life and I discontinued my studies.

People can actually be consumed by the pride of life, the lust of the flesh or the lust of the eyes. I once read of a rather grisly example that fits this self-consuming description. It has to do with the killing of a wolf.

If an Eskimo wants to kill a wolf, he coats a knife with animal blood and lets it freeze. Then he coats it with more animal blood and freezes it again. The procedure is repeated a number of times, until the entire knife is covered and coated by frozen animal blood. Then the knife is planted, blade up, in the snow at night.

A wolf will smell this blood from a considerable distance away, locate the knife and begin licking. As the wolf licks harder and faster, the sharp blade becomes exposed, but the wolf doesn't notice the sting or his own tongue being cut. The wolf's appetite for blood is so great he doesn't realize his own blood is mixed with it. His appetite drives him to lick more and more, until the morning finds him dead—a victim of his own lusts.

Could anything more graphic describe what happens to humans who don't learn to check their thirst? The great illusion is that we can become satisfied on our own.

The Truth

What is the truth about satisfaction? If it's selfish, it won't ultimately satisfy. The apostle John had it down well: "The world passes away and the lusts of it, but he who does the will of God abides forever."[5]

We come to realize that only when we are in God and in God's will are we satisfied. The prophet Isaiah, speaking for God, shows us how to turn from dissatisfaction to ultimate satisfaction:

> Why do you spend money for that which is not bread and you labor for that which satisfies not? Hearken diligently unto me and eat that which is good and let your soul delight itself in fatness.[6]

Soul food. Real soul food comes when you learn to stop radically pursuing selfish pleasures and hearken (listen) to God.

The only glimpse we have of Jesus as a teenager was at age twelve, when He was asking questions in the temple. When asked what He was doing there, He replied that He was "about [His] Father's business." This is what gives great satisfaction—to be about God's business.

It is one of the great paradoxes of Christianity that to gain your life, you lose it. To obtain life, you have to give it away.

I was in a Bible study one noontime at the hospital in Fort Campbell, Kentucky. A young woman who was married to a Marine private was in the group that day. She described how they lived on a meager income and had allotted thirty dollars for that week's groceries. As they arrived at the grocery store, they noticed a homeless man, badly in need of a bath, sitting outside. Everyone was stepping around him and avoiding eye contact. Something clicked inside them, and at the same moment, they were each compelled to give their week's grocery money to the homeless man, who received it with a surprised, grateful grin. They didn't know exactly what they'd be eating this next week, but their cupboards weren't bare and they were confident they'd get by.

As they walked into their apartment, the telephone was ringing. It was the base commissary (grocery store) calling to say they'd won a two-hundred dollar gift certificate!

See, that's how it works. You give, and it's given back to you eventually. You love, and love works its way around to you. Not only will those benefits come your way; you're also more likely to be healthier and live longer. Dr. Kenneth Cooper says, "We don't die. We kill ourselves."

Consider the five major causes of death for people who die prematurely between the ages of thirty-five and fifty-four:

	Men	Women
1.	heart attacks	breast cancer
2.	lung cancer	heart attacks
3.	auto accidents	stroke
4.	cirrhosis of the liver	auto accidents
5.	stroke	cirrhosis of the liver

Studies show that people who regularly attend church once a week live longer, have fewer health problems, lower blood pressure and better marriages. The list goes on and on.

If you want satisfaction and the good things in this life, you best find it through God. The person who gives his or her life to God gets it back a hundredfold.

Then you shall know the truth and the truth shall set you free.

—JOHN 8:32, NIV

Progress is impossible without change; and those who cannot change their minds cannot change anything.

—GEORGE BERNARD SHAW

I always wanted to be somebody, but I should have been more specific.

—ANONYMOUS

As long as a man willingly accepts himself, he will continue to grow and develop his potentialities. As long as he does not accept himself, much of his energies will be used to defend rather than explore and actualize himself.

—RALPH WALDO EMERSON

The unexamined life is not worth living.

—SOCRATES

Psychotherapy will put a bandage on the gash; but for healing, men's lives must be changed from within.

—RAYMOND LARSON

You can't change circumstances and you can't change other people, but you can let God change you.

—EVELYN CHRISTENSON

When I came to believe in Christ's teaching, I ceased desiring what I had wished for before. The direction of my life, my desires became different. What was good and bad changed places.

—LEO TOLSTOY

Can I Change?

"Maps, scripts, and Holy Writ"

$\mathcal{M}$ ost of us resist change. We are creatures of habit who become set in our ways, even comfortable in our familiar dysfunctional behavior. The truth is, though, that change goes on all around us. Whether we like it or not, it happens. I'm sure, when Adam and Eve were being ushered out of the Garden of Eden, that Adam turned to Eve and remarked, "Honey, I think we're going through a period of transition."

In this regard, we're a little like the turtle mugged by a gang of snails. When the police arrived at the crime scene, they asked what had occurred in the turtle's encounter with the snail gang. He shrugged and said, "I don't know. It all happened too fast!"

The world is rapidly changing around us. And the greater question is not "will you change?" but "how will you change?"

The apostle Paul once penned these significant words: "Don't be conformed to this world, but be transformed by the renewing of your mind that you may prove what is the good and acceptable will of God."[1] Paul starts with a negative—don't be conformed to this world. You see, the world has other plans for you.

Think of the times you've talked to little children about their plans. Ask a child what he or she wants to be when all grown up. Rita Rudner comically comments that adults are always asking kids what they're going to do when they grow up because adults are still looking for ideas themselves!

Notice that children have big thoughts. They want to be famous singers or athletes or actors or doctors. Then, what happens to most of us is that somebody comes along and rains on our parade. Someone tells us we can't do this or that because of our background, gender, ethnicity, education—or any number of pitiful excuses.

People decide for us. Cruel and erroneous assessments are made regarding our ability. We're put in boxes of a sort and often stifled there. And most sadly of all, we too frequently buy into these scripts and inaccurate beliefs.

In the introduction of this book, you were asked to think of your life as a movie. There is a term borrowed from psychology called *scripting* that develops this theme. If your life is a movie, you are following a script. The directors are often parents or other significant people who've impacted your life. We are "scripted" early in our lives.

But here's a beautiful thought about scripts that we don't often realize—scripts can be changed! It's *your* life now. This is your chapter of the family history. Many of you readers have begun to do just that. You're breaking away from old preconceived perceptions about your ability and potential, and beginning to make major changes.

You may be a little like the woodpecker who flew away from his home in the forest. Perched on the side of a tree, he decided to start his work on a certain spot. Just as he made contact with the tree, a bolt of lightening split the tree from top to bottom, knocking the woodpecker to the ground. He picked himself up and smoothed his feathers, exclaiming, "A fellow doesn't realize what he can do until he gets away from home!"

A couple years ago, William Murray, son of deceased atheist

activist Madalyn Murray-O'Hair, gave his testimony at my home church. William Murray was scripted by his mother to be an atheist. Indeed, his mother was the most prominent atheist in the country and tried to eradicate religion from public schools. Her son was supposed to be an atheist just like her. But God had other plans. Today, Willam Murray is a son of the living God, a believer in Jesus Christ, a minister and well-known speaker.

I once had a favorite student in my university classes. She came to school later in life. She had quit high school and run away from home to escape an oppressive household where she was expected to wait on her father and brothers hand and foot. That's how women were viewed in that household. She was always told, "You're pretty, but you're not too smart." If you hear those kind of comments all your life, you become scripted. You believe it. She did.

She went on to raise a family of her own. When the children were all school-aged, she began to think about changing her script. She'd always felt cheated over her lack of education, but had remained a voracious reader in all kinds of fields of study. Against her entire family's advice, she went on to earn a GED. Next was an application to the local college, which required an entrance exam. Because her admission was contingent upon a good A.C.T. score, she studied hard in preparation. When the scores came back, she had attained a thirty-six—a perfect score.

When I heard about this remarkable woman, I knew I had to seek her out and interview her. That's how I got this story. I asked if getting a perfect score on the A.C.T. had changed her perception of herself and her script. She smiled and replied, "My family only had it half-right. I'm not only pretty… I'm smart, too." She went on to graduate with honors and was offered an outstanding job with a good salary at a large firm. That was God working within her. She had decided to "not be conformed," but rather be "transformed by the renewing of [her] mind."

There's another term I like that was first presented to me in M. Scott Peck's book, *The Road Less Traveled.* He uses a phrase called "mapping" for how you navigate through your world.[2]

Physical maps are the way we see the structure of the world. Psychological maps are the way we see our personal worlds. They tell us:

- Where we're supposed to go
- What we're supposed to be doing
- What other people are like and how to respond to them
- Our philosophy of life.

And just as physical maps change over time—think of all the changing nations in the Balkans or Africa—so do our inner maps. Albert Ellis would say that the world is your mirror. In other words, you'll see the world in ways that will validate your world view.

- If you believe you're not capable, you'll find evidence for it.
- If you want to believe nobody loves you or cares for you, you'll convince yourself it's true.

The world is your mirror; your map.

When I completed my first graduate program, I took a job at a state university. In my first year I did a lot of counseling, but I especially remember four frustrating cases, all young women with similar problems. These young women were convinced they were fat. Their problem was labeled anorexia, and two of the girls were bulimic as well. The bulimic girls would not only self-starve, but would go on binge-eating episodes and then either regurgitate it all by tickling their throats or hustle it through their systems with heavy use of laxatives.

This is somewhat common in our culture for young women. My clients, as children, all played with Barbie dolls. They watched television programs featuring paper-thin models and dancers. With all these images, the fat was actually in their heads.

I spent a great amount of time counseling one young woman, an attractive twenty-year-old senior. Instead of going out with friends on a Friday night, she would rent a room at a local hotel. Then she would go to a local grocery store and eat everything that, as a dancer, she wasn't supposed to—like big, chewy loaves of bread and pound bags of chocolate. She would eat it all in the room while watching HBO and then throw it up in the bathroom. She'd regurgitated in this manner so many times that stomach acid from the upheavals had worn some of the enamel off her pretty teeth.

The amazing thing was none of these girls was actually fat. Each just believed it. It was their map, their world view.

Renewing Your Mind

In truth it's very hard to get people to revise their maps. In order to truly change, you start with your mind. People have ideals in their heads, a sense of utopia. Actually the Greek word for utopia means "no place." There *is* no perfect place or standard on earth. There is only a perfect God who is perfectly capable of changing us. And when God changes our minds, our maps change with it.

At age forty, Charles Colson was special consul to Richard Nixon, President of the United States. Then came the Watergate scandal, a humiliating trial and a prison sentence. The pain drove him to God. There, in prison, he observed the other prisoners' behavior. Some would sleep whenever they could to escape from reality. Others constantly watched television. Some would just emit a vacant stare for hours. Colson came to realize that, for these men, prison didn't just surround them. Prison had gotten *inside* of them. Prison had become their map. They were enslaved within.

One day, helpless with despair in realizing he couldn't change himself, Charles Colson fully gave in to the one force, the one person who *could* change him—God, through Jesus Christ! He became a radically changed man. His mind was renewed and transformed. As head of prison fellowship, he has helped thousands of prisoners to be freed from the walls within their minds as only God can do this work.

Adapting Your Behavior

Sometimes you can change your mind by practicing different behaviors. Many of us don't live our lives in the present. We're not really here in the now. We keep drifting back into the past and its accompanying behaviors.

Roger Bannister, an Englishman, was the first man to run a sub four-minute mile. The very next month, John Landy, an Australian, bettered the record by a second. Not long afterward, the two of them were competing in a track meet in British Columbia. They went neck-and-neck for most of the race. As they entered the final lap, Landy pulled out ahead, but he couldn't see Bannister. As the finish line came into sight, Landy looked back to see where Bannister was. Bannister surged by him and won the race. Landy later told reporters, "If I hadn't looked back, I would have won the race."

Sometimes we miss the best in life because we're too busy looking back. The apostle Paul wrote, "Forgetting that which is behind and straining towards what is ahead, I press on toward the goal to win the prize for which God has called me."[3]

Intentionally practice behaviors that will keep you in the present, which is the only real time God has given you. Paradoxically, part of how we do this is by having a (future) goal for how we want to be. Picture yourself as being competent, and then act that way. Think of negative behaviors you practice and would like to rid yourself of during the next year.

In early adulthood, I developed a mild fear of heights. I wasn't afraid to be in high places; I just didn't want to be anywhere near the edge. I didn't like this fear, but had learned to accept it. My family and I were in downtown Atlanta on vacation. We went for lunch at the Westin Hotel, which has a restaurant on top of its seventy-two-story cylindrical structure. We got into a glass elevator and it took us up seventy-two stories on the outside of the building.

As we slowly climbed the outside of the huge building, everyone was commenting on the view, the distance (the people looked like ants!) and how cool it was to be hanging outside of the hotel. My palms got all sweaty and I was clutching the railing much more tightly than usual. By the time we got to the top, I had sweat through my shirt.

Then and there I decided I didn't want this fear to be a part of my life anymore. On my family's yearly summer pilgrimage to a large amusement park, I determined to ride every single roller coaster—and I'm glad that I did, with the exception of one where the lines were too long. I realized I could handle anything for three minutes, and by the end was actually somewhat enjoying myself.

The same is true in the spiritual realm. When you want to go to new heights (and God is always there helping you to do this), you feel uncomfortable. You're nervous. You're not used to these new behaviors, not always happy about it at the same time. But afterwards, you're glad you went along for the ride.

When you intentionally change your patterns of behavior over time, the Holy Spirit comes alongside of you and helps you. In fact, the Greek term for Holy Spirit is the Paraclete, and it refers to the coming alongside of you when you need assistance. As you step into your better self, you start to actually become that way.

Have a Heart

A changed mind. Changed behaviors. Each are significant, but of paramount importance is a changed heart. To some degree, through the force of your own will, you can change thoughts, attitudes and actions. That's how God designed you. However, you can't change your heart, which is the will, the seat of emotions and drives.

A motion picture that touched me deeply was *Saving Private Ryan*. There is a scene where, as an old man, Private Ryan visits the gravesites of those who sacrificed their lives to protect him. He falls on his knees and tearfully looks up to ask his wife, "Have I been a decent man? Have I led a decent life?"

It's a question we should all ask, for intrinsically we seem to know, deep within ourselves, that it's not all about the externals. It's not about appearance, possessions or success. It's about the interior life. A matter of the heart. Am I a decent person—have I lived a decent life?

David, the psalmist, once prayed, "Create in me a clean heart O God and renew a right spirit within me."[4] Without God, you don't have a clean heart. Your interior life is dirty. It is an unwashed heart. And you can't clean it up on your own. You can't change it through force of will.

How *does* one get it clean, then? By an act the Bible refers to as repentance. You feel sorrow; you acknowledge you've been doing it your way—the wrong way—and you turn to God through Jesus Christ. A person who does this gains solutions and also inherits a new perspective on life because the heart is changed.

Jesus said, "Blessed are the pure in heart for they shall *see* God." Only when your heart becomes pure, only when it is cleansed, can you see God. God was always there. You just had trouble seeing Him. It's like a time when perhaps you were driving a car and it was hard to see through the windshield because it was dirty. You sprayed a bunch of washer fluid and ran the windshield wipers like mad, but you still couldn't see out. Then you came to realize that the smudge and dirtiness was on the *inside* of the windshield.

That's what it's like when your interior life is dirty. When it's cleansed from the inside, your view towards the outside is changed. You notice things you've never seen before. For example, if while sitting reading this book, you look around for a half-dozen items in the room with the color green in them, you will quickly notice things you never observed before. A green book, green in the couch, a green painting. This is because you're operating out of a "green mindset."

When your interior is changed to a God mindset, suddenly you see God everywhere. And more importantly, people even start to see God in you.

A couple took their son with them to Europe, where they toured many great cathedrals. Upon arriving home, the little boy's Sunday-school teacher asked him if he'd learned what a saint was. The boy remembered the many cathedrals with the stained glass windows depicting famous Christian saints and he replied, "Oh, yes. A saint is a person whom the light shines through." What a terrific way to describe someone who has had his or her heart cleansed by God! An inner purity and beauty radiates through such a person.

There is a goodness present now. It is an imputed goodness. A work done supernaturally by God through the Holy Spirit.

Yes, a person can change—with God's help. God is a God of second chances and will transform lives. Another favorite old movie of mine, *City Slickers,* struck a cord with aging baby boomers searching for meaning in life, but anyone could enjoy it. There's a point in the movie when one of the central characters has messed up his marriage, his job and life in general, and he's deeply discouraged. One of his buddies speaks a profoundly comforting and true line: "Hey. Life's a do-over."

Life *is* a do-over. We can make significant changes for the better. And that is very good news.

If we have our own why of life we can bear almost any how.

—Friedrich Nietzsche

If you learn from defeat you really haven't lost.

—Zig Zigler

All things work together for the good of them that love God and are called according to His purpose.

—Romans 8:28, Paraphrased

Things alter for the worse spontaneously, if they are not altered for the better designedly.

—Francis Bacon

It's not the load that breaks you down; it's the way you carry it.

—Lena Horne

Look toward the sun and the shadows will fall behind you.

—Sundial in Sussex, England

The first thing to do when you have made a mistake is not to give up doing what you were doing and start something altogether new, but to start over again with the thing you began badly and try, for the love of God, to do it well.

—Thomas Morton

Call on God, but row away from the rocks.

—Indian Proverb

The event has detrivialized our society. In shockingly graphic terms, it has caused people to ask what is really important in life. They are running to the church for answers.

—Darrell Bock on 9/11/01

How Can I Handle Life's Adversities?

"A bend in the road is not the end of the road"

*E*ach of us lives in what could be called our own "assumptive world." We assume the world works in a specific way. When things don't go according to plan in our own minds, it throws us into confusion, denial and anger. Here are some common assumptions:

Invulnerability—we believe that serious problems won't happen to us. Trauma quickly shatters this belief.

Justice—we expect the work to be fair and just, when in fact much of the time it is not.

Control—we somehow think that, through doing all the right things, we can control people and circumstances (we can't for long).

Personal Identity—much of what we understand about ourselves comes in relation to others. When we lose a loved one, it's a loss of identity. When we lose a job or retire, it's a loss of identity.

There are many other assumptions we make. The point is you operate out of a working belief system and it impacts your reaction to negative events in your life.

A Bible Example

Joseph is one of the most beloved characters in the Bible. One reason why he was so special was his response to great difficulties that occurred to him. Every time he was knocked down, he got up again with sustained faith in God.

Joseph's adventures would have crippled a lesser man. His jealous, scheming brothers sought to kill him, then sold Joseph into slavery instead. While a slave in Egypt, he rose to prominence in his master's household, but was unjustly accused of making a pass at the master's wife and thrown into prison.

In prison, Joseph assisted others with dream interpretation and was promised help with his case, but was forgotten and left in the dungeon. Finally, he was remembered and summoned to interpret the Pharaoh's dream, resulting in a promotion that leapfrogged him to the highest place in the land under Pharaoh. He saved the nation from famine, and when his brothers come for a distance to buy grain, he was united with his family.

Joseph could have been bitter. He had every human reason to be angry and full of vengeance. Instead, he said to his brothers, "Even though you intended to do harm to me, God intended it for good."[1] Joseph saw beyond the circumstances around him to see what God was doing.

There is something so attractive about a person like Joseph, who stays pure and devoted to God despite experiencing extreme tribulations. He displayed a wisdom in looking at life "over the long haul."

The Wisdom to Perceive

Joseph was a wise man. He perceived that the strange and difficult times in his life had a purpose. Perspective changes everything. Joseph was trying to see life from another angle.

Speed skater Dan Jansen suffered a whole series of disappointments in three consecutive Olympics before winning the gold medal on his fourth try. He kept his sense of perspective by remembering an incident at the speed skating national championships when he was but nine years old. A slight slip on a turn caused him to lose the national championship by a single point and he cried in his parents' car for the whole six-hour trip home. Upon entering the driveway, his father said gently, "You know, Dan, there's more to life than skating around in a circle."

The wisdom to perceive. The ability to understand that even in defeat you can leave lessons and become stronger than ever.

A minister once spoke about spending a day working with his father-in-law, a farmer in Kansas. Together as they worked, they discussed the differences in city life and farm life.

His father-in-law philosophized, "The biggest difference I see is that city people expect each year to be better than the last. If they haven't gotten a raise, acquired something new or found themselves somehow better off, they're dissatisfied.

"On the farm, you don't expect the fields to yield more each year. You expect good years and bad. You can't control the weather and you pray you avoid disaster. You work hard and accept what comes."

Troubles can traumatize us or energize us spiritually. David, the psalmist, prayed to God and said, "God, you have *enlarged* me in my distress."[2] The word "enlarged" here means to be large and spacious, like a chamber. You become a bigger person. You start to see the wide perspectives. Solomon has this largeness of heart—a special wisdom that sees things as God sees them.[3]

The Psalms note that God especially seems to enlarge us in times of distress. How does it work that way? Apparently, when things go well for us all the time, we can become spiritually apathetic and lackadaisical about necessary holy habits. But insert some distress into life, and we quickly realize our own confidence, cleverness, power and our own inadequate philosophies can't carry us through every personal crisis. And in that moment, we may turn back to God.

Charles Beard once wrote, "When it's dark enough, you can see stars." Paradoxically, when it's really dark enough, you can begin to see God.

When I was twenty-three years old, my best friend was killed in a car accident. I was distressed and in deep emotional pain. There was nothing in the world I could do to bring James back to life. I knew that James had eternal life with Christ, but the shock of grief hit me hard.

After the funeral service, James' brother, a Naval Academy Midshipman, showed me a verse from the Bible that comforted me. Psalms 116:15 said, "Precious in the sight of the Lord is the death of His saints." Later I read that "the Lord comes nigh unto the broken-hearted."4 That's what happened in my distress. I got a new perspective and God came nigh unto me. God is especially close to those who are suffering.

Many of you reading these words right now have experienced such deep grief you can scarcely express it. All of you have been through a dark time of personal crisis where you inwardly cried out, "O, God, this hurts so badly. This rejection, this injustice, this illness, this change is too much for me."

You know what God wants to do with you as a result of that incident? God wants to enlarge you. The psalmist writes of "God lifting His countenance upon you."5 God desires to illuminate you and make your face shine as a conqueror even through your tears. Only God can do that.

An entire nation went through this level of crisis on September 11, 2001. The pain and suffering generated can make us or break us as a people.

The Courage to Believe

It takes courage to believe in God's beneficent plan even as you are suffering. Oberlin, the French pastor, was comforting a woman in distress. He used an illustration. Oberlin said,

> Dear lady, I have before me two stones, alike in color, of the same water, clear, pure and clean. Yet there is a marked difference. One has a dazzling brilliance. The other is quite dull. Why? Because one has received eighty cuts and the other only eight. The stone that has suffered much is brilliant; the one that has suffered little is dim and lusterless.

Ralph Erskine, who suffered greatly with physical illness late in life, wrote, "I have known more of God since I came to this bed than through all my life." That's because God comes nigh unto the brokenhearted. When you're hurting, God is close by.

God is a big God. And when we're close to God, we change in His presence. Like Moses, our faces will shine in the light of His countenance upon us. And we will rise above the difficulties of our lives.

Norman Vincent Peale has pointed out that when a storm strikes an eagle, he sets his wings in such a way that the air currents send him above the storm by their very fury. As a result of being with God, *you* rise above the fray. God not only enlarges your heart; God enlarges your steps as well.[6] This means you walk confidently in the midst of turmoil and difficulties.

Abraham Lincoln saw things this way. No American president went through more suffering—personally or nationally—while in office. While a younger man, after losing yet another Senate race (he lost many political races), he wrote,

The path was worn and slippery. My foot slipped from under me, knocking the other out of the way, but I recovered and said to myself, "It's a slip... and not a fall."

Just a slip, friends. A bend in the road is not the end of the road. God enlarges your steps and gives you confidence.

As a boy, I grew up in Wisconsin. In the wintertime it was difficult for a child to walk on the snow which was several feet deep. Once I borrowed a pair of snowshoes and was amazed how I could walk right on top of snowdrifts that could have buried me up to my neck. Instead, I was on top of it all!

The spiritual analogy is clear. God enlarges your steps to help you stay on top of things. The Psalmist wrote that he was enlarged in his distress and came to realize his first steps (and ours) are to be back to God.

One snowy Wisconsin morning when I was ten years old, I was riding the bus to school. As the driver attempted to turn the bus around in a cul-de-sac, it became stuck in a snowdrift. All the children had to get off the bus and I was just standing around, not watching what was going on. I heard a child yell at me and turned to see that our school bus had lurched violently out of the snowdrift and was backing right into me. It was only a few feet from me at that point and I spontaneously just fell backwards onto a pile of wood as the bus bumper backed over the whole length of my body. It was just about to crush my head and then the bus stopped suddenly in response to the other children's screams.

As the bumper eased off me, I realized it had pulled muscles in my body in both directions—coming and going. I felt sore and stretched out, like the Rubber Band Man.

I wasn't hurt badly, but it was a close encounter. Over the next several days I would sometimes just find my tears flowing uncontrollably as I thought about my brush with death.

Shortly thereafter, I walked to the front of a movie theater at a Billy Graham evangelistic event in response to an invitation to accept Jesus Christ as Savior and Lord. I had been enlarged in my distress and it led me to take those steps towards God. I finally had the courage to believe.

The Persistence to Succeed

Two announcers were covering a football game between the Chicago Bears and the New York Giants in the 1980s. One announcer observed that Walter Payton, the Bears' all-star half-back, had accumulated over nine miles in career rushing yardage. The other announcer responded, "Yeah, and that's with someone knocking him down every 4.6 yards!"

One of the great strengths of early Christianity was its perseverance in light of enormous opposition. This comes with the package in trying to follow Jesus Christ.

Even a cursory reading of the New Testament Gospels reveals how Jesus was constantly facing difficulties. In fact, he even told his disciples to expect troubles, but to be of good cheer because He would help them overcome.[7]

When the Army of Israel would go out to battle against its enemies, it would send out a team of musicians ahead of the soldiers. The musicians would play their instruments and sing praises to God, thanking Him for a victory. What an act of faith! What an "in your face" deed to perform in the presence of your enemies! The Israelites perceived God's favor, believed God's power and went on to succeed in battle.

Have you come to realize that personal battles just come with the package? Paul wrote to his young disciple, Timothy, these words: "In fact, everyone who wants to live a godly life in Christ Jesus will be persecuted" (2 Timothy 3:12, NKJV).

No ifs, ands or buts about it. Trials *will* come your way.

Brother Andrew, who'd smuggled Bibles into countries for many years, told of an East European minister who was speaking in the United States. This man had suffered greatly for his faith. He had been tortured. He had been imprisoned. And as is often the case with one who has been imprisoned for a long time, he didn't say much.

Some in the audience seemed to think the minister was backwards and behind the times. One woman in the audience whispered, "He sure doesn't say much." Her companion whispered back, "When you hang on a cross… you don't need to say much."

When James Calvert went out to the cannibal Fiji islands with the message of the gospel, the captain of the ship on which he traveled sought to dissuade him: "You will risk your life and all those with you if you go among these savages."

Calvert's reply: "We died before we came here."

Jim Elliot, the martyred missionary wrote in his diary, "He is no fool who gives what he cannot keep to gain what he cannot lose."

There is an awesome persistence among those who have rightly aligned their life plans with the will of God. My own life verse is Romans 8:28—"All things work together for the good of those who love God and are called according to His purpose." It doesn't say all things are good, just that all things work together to bring about good in the end. That is why Paul wrote to the Thessalonian church to "give thanks in all circumstances, for this is God's will."[8] Not thanks *for* all things but *in* all things.

A victorious attitude of praise and thanks to God will help you overcome any negative events in your life. Make a decision to "let go and let God" help you take control of whatever situation in which you find yourself, and you will discover a dramatic difference.

Anybody who thinks that morality can be viewed as purely a private affair, a matter of individual opinion, a matter of what feels right for me, is in my opinion, deluded.

—ARCHBISHOP OF CANTERBURY GEORGE CAREY

A little philosophy inclines a man's mind to atheism; but depth in philosophy brings a man's mind to religion.

—SIR FRANCIS BACON

Not to be fortified with good ideas is to be victimized by bad ones.

—CARL F.H. HENRY

I will walk about in freedom for I have sought your precepts.

—PSALM 119:45, NIV

We cannot break God's laws—but we can break ourselves against them.

—A. MAUDE ROYDEN

The moral life of any people rises or falls with the vitality or decay of its religious life.

—JOHN SUTHERLAND BONNELL

He who spits at Heaven, it falls in his face.

—ANONYMOUS

Why Be Good?

"Morality-mart"

The Great Wall of China is an awe-inspiring sight. Built by the ancient Chinese to protect themselves from invading hordes, it stretches for fifteen hundred miles. At various places the wall is between twelve to forty feet wide and twenty to fifty feet high. It was to be a significant deterrent to any potential enemy.

However, in the first one hundred years of the wall's existence, the nation of China was invaded three times. How could this be? Their enemies simply bribed the gatekeepers and easily marched on in through a gate.

Character counts. Morality matters in any nation. No matter how militarily powerful or economically strong any country is, it depends on the basic morality of its people—or it eventually ceases to exist as a nation.

Truth Decay

The United States, great country that it may be, is a civilization in decline. People are living much longer and have become so used to our present existence that we have begun to think the "poison culture" is normal.

What is normal now, in early twenty-first century America?

- Outside of nations at civil war, we are the most crime-ridden nation on the face of the earth.

- Every day, over ninety Americans successfully commit suicide. Many hundreds more attempt it unsuccessfully.

- Our sexual assault rate is eight times higher than any other nation that keeps such statistics. Our robbery rate exceeds the next nearest nation's six fold.

- One third of the births in this country are to unwed mothers (That's up from five percent in 1960).

- Far and away the greatest cause of injury to American women is being beaten up by their husbands and boyfriends.

- According to the Center for Disease Control, every single day thirty-three thousand Americans contract a sexually transmitted disease. That's twelve million Americans a year.

Over twenty-five years ago, when Aleksandr Solzhenitsyn was speaking at Harvard University, he referred to America as "morally exhausted." More concerned with rights… than with what is right. Life, liberty, and the pursuit to destroy ourselves. Utilizing Senator Patrick Moynihan's oft-quoted phrase, we have "defined deviancy downward" and resignedly accepted life in a dysfunctional culture. We are experiencing a morality meltdown.

And no, it hasn't always been like this. Not that there was ever a perfect time in American culture—there never was. But it was not very long ago in history that couples wed for life, children were generally safe to play in the streets and religion was considered an integral part of the public sphere.

My, how things have changed, with the United States leading

the world in divorces, child abuse a blight throughout the land and religion squeezed by the courts into a neutral corner.

A Cut-Flower Civilization

Eminent historian Will Durant, an honest humanist, once said in an interview:

> Moreover, we shall find it no easy task to mold a natural ethic strong enough to maintain moral restraint and social order without the support of supernatural consolations, hopes and fears. There is no significant example in history, before our time, of a society successfully maintaining moral life without the aid of religion.[1]

Durant had it right. Though admittedly not a religious man, his exhaustive scholarly studies of great civilizations led him to the conclusion that when religious influence is divorced from morality, a nation begins to fall apart.

Indeed, without God and a religion, *why be good?* Why obey any law at all?

Go back in time a few decades and beyond, and the most common answer you'd hear would have a strong religious component. God would be mentioned. Words like *sin, restraint, judgment* and *afterlife* would show up.

An often-forgotten line from John F. Kennedy's great inaugural speech says, "The rights of man come not from the generosity of the state, but from the hand of God." Forty years later, a president would be vilified for such a philosophy.

Or go back further into time. How did the country's founders view this issue? Francis Schaeffer notes:

> Think of this great flaming phrase: "certain inalienable rights." Who gives the rights? The state? Then they are not

inalienable, because the state can change them and take them away. Where do the rights come from? They understand that they were founding the country upon the concept that goes back into the Judeo-Christian thinking that there is someone there who gave the inalienable rights. Another phrase also stood there: "In God we trust." With this there is no confusion of what they were talking about. They publicly recognized that law could be king because there was a Law Giver, a Person to give the inalienable rights.[2]

It was this belief system that gave shape and substance to a developing nation. Now, that same nation is crowding religion to the periphery.

Elton Trueblood's prophetic word from the 1950s is coming true. He said we are becoming a "cut-flower civilization. As beautiful as cut flowers may be, they die because they are severed from their sustaining roots." We are slowly becoming severed from that which was foundational to a common moral ground.

Can We Be Good Without God?

Can we be good without God? The truth is we're not very good even with God.

History is replete with plenty of evidence of that. Scripture itself pulls no punches in displaying Bible character foibles.

Nonetheless, humans tend to think they are capable of operating just fine without any supernatural intervention. The Enlightenment period of history and the rise of humanism placed man at the center of the universe. While these philosophies have been around for centuries, it is only in the twentieth and now twenty-first century that the ideas were embraced wholesale by much of Western civilization, at least among academicians and politicians.

The world view can be summed up as secularism. Ravi Zacharias describes it as:

> The hard reality of choice for American intellectual and political life. Any view that affirms the supernatural is, by definition, considered irrelevant or irrational. Secularism or "saeculum" is implicitly "this worldly."[3]

Sociologist Peter Berger defines secularization as "the process by which sectors of society and culture are removed from the domination of religious institutions and symbols."[4] Secular philosophy has come to dominate and bully public university thought-life. To speak from a theistic framework—or God forbid, from a Christian perspective—is to be set up for ridicule. Zacharias notes that

> not surprisingly, therefore, students entering college are very guarded about their religious beliefs for fear of being outcasts in the world of learning.[5]

Alan Bloom, in *The Closing of the American Mind*, noted that college students rarely ask questions anymore. It isn't that students don't have the questions. It isn't that students aren't as bright as ever. Students are simply stymied by a prevailing philosophy in the classroom that shuts out the very deepest soul-searching question humans could ask.

Salad-Bar Faith

The unworkableness of this philosophy should be evident, though professors, media minds and others continue to promulgate their ideas from current positions of power. In response, an equally unworkable belief system has arisen that is very American and very Western in its attraction, although the roots are from the Far East, particularly Buddhism. It is the belief system that you get to choose your own faith. You get to create God as you see fit, in a kind of syncretistic spirituality. It's for people who recognize there is a spirit and a Divine being (*DUH!*) but wish to make up their own definition.

If you ever heard someone say, "Oh, I'm not religious—I'm spiritual," you may well have met a spiritual syncretist. Typically, baby boomers are the majority group. Wade Clark Roof's thorough study of the baby boomers' spiritual marketplace aptly describes them. He writes:

> "How can I feel good about myself?" emerged as a far more pressing question to many Americans than, "How can I be saved?" American boomers want community, but on strictly individual terms. They want human closeness without feeling cramped or obligated. They want a personal God who doesn't ask much personally. They want mystery, but in a controlled, non-disruptive way. They want a faith that's fulfilling, practical, earthy, tolerant, transcendent, fun, empowering, morally serious without being morally demanding, a faith that restores wonder and deepens intimacy and they want it to not ask too much or take up too much time.[6]

What happens is that the term "spiritual" can mean anything or everything or nothing. In fact, it is simply a catch-all phrase that allows one to pull God into the picture without any moral demands or church-community obligation. It is for the person who wants to believe in a higher power, but not submit to a higher authority.

It reflects a salad-bar approach to faith. One can pick or choose doctrine that feels good. It is substituting self-centered feeling over any organized religion. In fact, nearly half of the people interviewed in Roof's survey believed that all religions were equally good and true. This is a non-thinking, non-discriminating response if there ever was one.

Where does this sort of muddled thinking lead us? A twenty-four-year-old prostitute in White Pine County, Nevada, was interviewed by *Life* magazine regarding her relationship and communication with God.

"I don't think about my feelings a lot. [*She said*]. Instead I lie in bed and think onto him. I meditate because sometimes my words don't come out right. But he can find me. He can find what's inside of me just by listening to my thoughts. I ask him to help me and keep me going.

"A lot of people think working girls don't have any morals, any religion. But I do. I don't steal. I don't lie. The way I look at it, I'm not sinning. He's not going to judge me. I don't think God judges anybody."7

You get to create "god" in your own mind. It's why Steve Harper has claimed that "the present generation is lost on the sea of rampant subjectivism and excessive individualism." How different from people of the Bible, who believed in objective truth as when Moses said to Aaron, "You must distinguish between the holy and the common; between the unclean and clean."8 Traditional Christianity, as Leighton Ford has claimed, believes that Jesus Christ is not an addition, but an alternative. He is not considered just part of life, but the way, truth and life.

A Cracked Compass

Imagine a game devoid of rules and people get to make them up as they go along. That's how many people play at the game of life. No wonder it's so frustrating for them and for the people with whom they live and work. Even in this atmosphere of a subjective, feel-good search for meaning, some rules will inevitably rise to the forefront. William Watkins refers to these as "the new absolutes."9

The dominant new absolute philosophy proposes there are no absolutes. The proper name for this philosophy is _relativism._ Watkins defines this term:

> In short, relativism is the belief that truth and error, right and wrong, beautiful and ugly, normal and abnormal, and a host of other judgments are determined by the individual, her circumstances, or her culture, reality and morality and personal or social constrictions or both.[10]

When you hear people make such statements as:
What's true for you may not be true for me
It just totally depends on the situation
All religions are essentially the same
One person's art is another's pornography,
You've probably met a budding relativist.

Relativists reject absolute truth. And it is the dominant philosophy among young adults. Seventy-eight percent of Americans born between 1965 and 1983 believe there is no absolute truth.[11]

Same Vocabulary, Different Dictionary

Words are important not just because of symbolic value. Words make up a dialogue that enables persons with different viewpoints to have discussions in a civil fashion.

Significant words have come to characterize the philosophy of relativism. Indeed, they are a natural extension of the thought. Words such as _tolerance, pluralism, diversity,_ and _multiculturalism_ are all good words that have taken a decided twist for the twenty-first century.

All of these thoughts are found in the early Christian church. Jesus Himself stepped out of rigid social boundaries, claiming that all persons were special to God and that no one was favored because of gender, race or class.

The early church was an amazing experiment in tolerance, pluralism, multiculturalism and diversity. Former slaves sat in the same congregation as their former masters. Women were elevated to places of service and esteem. Neither class nor racial distinction held barriers anymore. To use the apostle Paul's words, "There is neither Jew nor Greek, slave nor free, male nor female, for you are all one in Christ Jesus."[12]

The church slowly changed Western civilization as we know it. D. James Kennedy has pointed out in his book, *What if Jesus Had Never Been Born?* that the entrance of Jesus' teaching into human history forever altered views of women, slavery, children, the poor, government, the sick, education, sexuality, science and art. In short, "Jesus Christ is the greatest man who ever lived—and most people don't know it."[13]

Relativism uses many of the same words as Christianity. But because the terms emanate from *post-modernism,* the same vocabulary is utilized with a different dictionary.

Charles Colson writes:

> Postmodernism rejects any notion of a universal, overarching truth and reduces all ideas to social constitutions shaped by class, gender and ethnicity. In postmodernism, all viewpoints, all lifestyles, all beliefs and behaviors are regarded as equally valid. Institutions of higher learning have embraced this philosophy so aggressively that they have adopted campus codes enforcing political correctness. Tolerance has become so important that no exception is tolerated.[14]

So, what's so dangerous about postmodernism? Why be concerned about its direction? Colson, who frequently speaks on university campuses, noted the impassive response of students to his provocative lectures:

Debate can be unpleasant at times, but at least it presupposes that there are truths worth defending, ideas worth fighting for. In our postmodernist age, however, your truths are yours, my truths are mine and none are significant enough to get passionate about. And if there is no truth, then we cannot persuade one another by rational arguments. All that's left is sheer power—which opens the door to a new form of fascism.[15]

Imposition of power. With the great fervency, new absolutes regarding beliefs about sexual preference, feminism, exclusion of religion, environmentalism and a host of uses are being hammered through court litigation into law. Oddly enough, the rallying cry often surrounds another good word, once again misused. This word is tolerance.

Doctrine by Opinion Poll

Tolerance is a wonderful virtue. It was surely practiced by Jesus Christ. Traditionally, it refers to "sympathy or indulgence for beliefs or practices from other than one's own."[16]

Kindness, acceptance, and understanding all are a part of tolerance. Even if you greatly differ with a person, you are still empathic and forbearing. This is part and parcel of the Christian ethos.

Josh McDowell persuasively argues that there now remains one word, but two meanings. He writes:

In contrast to traditional tolerance, which asserts that everyone has an equal right to believe or say what he thinks is right, the new tolerance—the way our children are being taught to believe—says that what every individual believes or says is equally right, equally valid. So not only does everyone have an equal right to his beliefs, but all beliefs are equal. All values are equal. All lifestyles are equal. All truth claims are equal.[17]

So do you believe this, tolerant reader? Do you believe we should respect the truth claims of racial supremacists like the Ku Klux Klan, or destructive militants like Timothy McVeigh or sexist macho men? I doubt if you respect the context of their beliefs—so all belief systems are neither right nor equal. Why aren't you tolerant of their practices?

The truth is that this new form of tolerance, present in our society, isn't even tolerant at all. William Watkins explains further:

The new tolerance is a natural corollary of the relativistic perspective. Since all truth and morals are up for grabs, the relativist must be a person committed to living out the new tolerance. This means she must be broad-minded, open to other beliefs, claims to truth, moral convictions, and different lifestyles. The tolerant person must make room for others to do as they wish even if their behavior contradicts or even mocks her own. The authentic relativist would not become upset when facing opposition to her views and she would never try to push her personal convictions on other people. Declaring anything right or wrong, true or false for anyone by herself would be unacceptable dare I say, a moral evil? Everyone must be left to live as they see fit. Live and let live. That is the summary maxim of the new virtue of tolerance.[18]

Watkins then asked if that's how tolerance is actually practiced:

No, not at all. In fact the very groups that claim to be advocates of new tolerance are not. The political correctness movement seeks to squelch what various groups view as offensive language behavior and perspectives. Multiculturalists seem bent on upholding the beliefs and practices of every other culture except those commended by Western civilization. Secularists are determined to keep religious expression out of the public arena. Pro-abortion and same-sex-rights activists march on city halls, run for public office and long to change or enact laws in order to gain legal and social sanctions for their personal views.[19]

Charles Colson has called this "the ugly side of tolerance." It has become a dialogue of the deaf. Who can shout down the other? How to gain the ear of a sympathetic judge or hire a persuasive lawyer to let your belief be imposed through law?

Do All Roads Lead to God?

How, then, does that impact religion and morality? Colson notes that "In today's relativistic environment, pluralism no longer means tolerating competing ideas, but rather forced neutrality; no one could offend another."[20]

Christianity is, by its very nature, offensive. People were so offended with Jesus' truth claims that they nailed Him to a cross. The cross is offensive and a stumbling block. Millions of Christian martyrs have been put to death because they didn't choose forced neutrality. They chose to die for the belief that Jesus Christ is the Son of God.

While Christianity is a marvelously inclusive faith, it has its own exclusiveness as well. Jesus said, "I am the way, the truth, and the life; no man comes unto the Father but by me."[21] The apostle John claimed that you must have a relationship with the Son of God to have life.[22] The writer of Acts records Peter as saying there is no name under earth by which a person could have salvation other than through Jesus Christ.[23] Jesus said the road to salvation was narrow and few would find it.[24]

The narrowness of this doctrine causes many persons to stumble. Yet it is clearly stated in the Bible and affirmed by church tradition over twenty centuries.

There have been some within the church, though, who have attempted to marry Christianity and a relativistic view of truth. Paul Little writes:

> ...It is clear that Christianity differs radically from other religions. We live in an age in which tolerance is a key word. Tolerance, however, must be clearly understood. Truth, by its very nature, is intolerant of error. If two plus two is four, the total at the same time cannot be twenty-three. But one is not regarded as intolerant because he disagrees with this answer and maintains the only correct answer is four. The same principle applies in religious matters. One must be tolerant of other points of view and respect their right to be heard. He cannot, however, be forced in the name of tolerance to agree that all points of view, including those that are mutually contradictory, are equally valid. Such a position is nonsense.[25]

Within Christianity, this contradictory doctrine has become known as universalism. Simply put, it means everybody gets to heaven. The emphasis is on the great love and compassion of God who could never judge or condemn one of His creatures.

The God of the Bible is kind, compassionate, merciful and forgiving. However, God is also just. If universalism is true and everybody gets to go to heaven, why be moral? Why send missionaries? Why bother to go to church or do service projects or any number of Christian acts?

The point is clear. Universalism does not fully represent God through Jesus Christ, who is patient with us, but does make moral demands.

What you believe about God will most definitely impact your personal morality. If you get to create God in your own mind, then you will create a moral infrastructure that will suit you. If you believe in the God of Christian history, as revealed in objective truth of Scripture, then you will search out those pages to find out how to live well.

Stay in Your Lane

The psalmist presents us with a paradox in moral boundaries when he writes: "I will walk about in freedom For I have sought out your precepts."[26]

Liberty can be found within borders. Boundaries can bring about freedom. Once, on television, I saw an unhappy activist shouting into the camera. In big letters on his tee-shirt were the words, "No Borders." Let me utilize a Cal Thomas term here. Such persons are actually moral phobic. They fear and reject an objective moral code. We live in a society hurling itself against any moral boundaries.

However, borders are there to protect us. God's very first recorded words to man were about boundaries. "Do not eat of the tree of the knowledge of good and evil."[27] These moral fences keep us from harm.

Billy Graham has commented that,

Moral law is more than a test for man's own good. Every law that God has given has been for man's benefit. If a man breaks it, he is not only rebelling against God, he is hurting himself.

You don't break God's laws when you step out of your lane; they break you. When you walk off a cliff into thin air, you don't prove the law of gravity. It's already there. You just prove you can't fly! The law of gravity was already in place whether you had discovered that truth or not.

Once, my impish, clever daughter came up to me and asked, "Dad, what was the highest point on the face of the earth before they discovered Mount Everest?" I replied, "I don't know, honey. What was the highest point on earth?" She smiled and said, "Mount Everest." See, the truth about Mount Everest being the highest point on the face of the earth was true whether or not we discovered it. We just have to appropriate it once we've been exposed to the truth.

The ancients referred to this as wisdom. Wisdom is accumulated knowledge and insight and, in this case, it is knowledge of God and God's laws.

As you try to make sense of the maze of choices and values, think of a puzzle. How do you recreate the pieces of a puzzle? You to start with the borders, the straight edges. Once you have the borders, it starts to come together in the center. Morality works much like this. As you submit yourself to the laws of faith clearly described in the Bible, you find yourself feeling more centered. Paradoxically, you feel greater freedom, for Jesus said the truth sets you free. You feel better about yourself. You feel a harmony with the universe because you've done the right thing.

I have had countless conversations with persons who made this decision. Once they chose to be obedient to the truths revealed in Scripture, they found a new, refreshing sense of life itself. They were indeed born again.

No temptation has seized you except what is common to men. And God is faithful: He will not let you be tempted beyond what you can bear. But when you are tempted, He will also provide a way out so that you can stand up under it.

—1 CORINTHIANS 10:13, NIV

The devil is always trying to trick us into extremes.

—C.S. LEWIS

My temptations have been my masters in divinity.

—MARTIN LUTHER

Most people who fly from temptation leave a forwarding address.

—ANONYMOUS

Temptation provokes me to look upward to God.

—JOHN BUNYAN

God is better served in resisting a temptation to evil than in many formal prayers.

—WILLIAM PENN

It's easier to stay out than get out.

—MARK TWAIN

It is one thing to be tempted, another thing to fall.

—WILLIAM SHAKESPEARE

Can I Overcome Temptation?

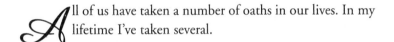

"Saying yes and no"

*A*ll of us have taken a number of oaths in our lives. In my lifetime I've taken several.

- As a child I repeated the pledge of allegiance to the flag.

- I stood before an Army officer at age eighteen and affirmed that I would support and defend the constitution of the United States against all enemies, foreign and domestic.

- I knelt at my ordination and vowed I would serve God through the authority of word, sacrament and order.

- I stood, knees shaking, at my wedding ceremony and pledged my life's loyalty to my wife.

Jesus once said to let your "yes be yes" and your "no be no."[1] Sticking by your commitments, saying "yes," is good for you. Saying "no" helps shape your identity. It defines who you are and what you stand for. Yes and no are the alternate heartbeats of Life. Yes-no. Yes-no. You say yes to what you need. You say no unto that which is not necessary.

Daniel, a famous Bible character, purposed how to act ahead of time in his heart.[2] In young adulthood, he decided what he stood for; then, when temptation came his way, he was able to stick with his convictions.

Do you have difficulty with temptation? Do you find it hard to say "no" even now that you're an adult? I always find that odd, since saying no was one of the first words you learned as a baby. It was a part of your natural development. You were creating a separate identity from your mother. It's something we all go through.

Toddlers say no a lot. Yet, when we become adults, we seem to have trouble saying it. Part of the reason is we've gone through a period of history where saying no was out of fashion. People want to define themselves as free, accepting, tolerant and open. We've lived so long by the neurotic need to say yes to everything—we've rubber-stamped so many morals, values and practices right by us— that we're unsure of ourselves. What do we say no to? An anonymous writer has said that if we haven't that within us which is above us, we shall soon yield to that which is around us.

Now, saying no on one level is really saying yes on yet another level. Sometimes when you say no to questionable or unhealthy activities or practices, you're really saying yes to God. You're saying, "Yes, God, I believe Your ways are right." And when you see it in this perspective, instead of life being a constant *negation*, it is a constant *affirmation* of the presence of an eternal, caring God.

In order to truly understand these concepts we'll first have to investigate the very nature of temptation itself.

The Nature of Temptation

Temptation cannot be understood without a reference to the "tempter." Within the context of Scripture, we're presented with a character known as Satan. There are many other names given to

136

this personification of evil in the Bible:

Angel of Light	Devil
Beelzebub	Roaring Lion
Accuser of the Brethren	Prince of the power of air
Evil One	Ruler of this world

Whatever tag you put on this face, it is real and it is powerful. I once heard a theologian say that if there's not a devil, then there's someone or something around that's a lot like him, creating terrible havoc in the world. Peter describes him "Like a roaring lion, walking about, seeking whom he may devour."[3] His personal attacks are described as "flaming arrows."[4]

But for all the havoc wreaked by him, he is not all-powerful. Jesus once comforted His disciples, saying that, "In the world you shall have tribulation, but be of good cheer for I have overcome the world."[5]

German theologian Emil Bruner once made the curious suggestion that Adolph Hitler should be posthumously given an honorary doctor of theology degree because he awakened Europe to her Christian heritage by showing her what the world would be like without Christianity.[6]

Temptation will occur. But temptation of itself is not a sin. Martin Luther once wrote that "We can't keep the birds from flying over our heads, but we can keep them from nesting in our hair." Temptations will fly all around us. Our responsibility is to not give in to them. How then, are we tempted? There are several commonalties to this process.

Doubt

Bobby Leach, an Englishman, once startled the world by going over Niagara Falls in a barrel. He came out unharmed. A few days later he slipped on an orange peel and fractured his leg. Note—it wasn't the big thing that injured him. It was the small thing that laid him flat.

For Christians, it's not the Niagaras that roar over us, it's the little whispers in our ears. In the Book of Genesis, Satan confronted Eve with a questioning process: "What did God really say?"[7] A seed of doubt was planted in Eve's mind.

The same strategy was employed in the temptation of Jesus. The devil came to Jesus and began with, "*If* you are the Son of God…"[8] First, he raised doubts; then came the temptations. He raises doubts in our mind: "Did God really say such and such a course of action is wrong?" He tries to undermine our confidence in what God has said and in our relationship with Him.[9]

Again, the doubt is not sin, if you choose to let faith rise up at that moment to conquer the questioning thought. Usually such thoughts are fleeting and can be quickly dismissed if we don't "let them nest in our hair."

Distraction

Temptation usually pulls us away from the things that are most important at the time. Sometimes the attraction has no purpose whatsoever. (May I mention mindless hours of television-watching here?) David, the psalmist, prayed to God to "Turn my eyes away from worthless things."[10]

It reminds me of those artificial lures that fishermen use. They look so unrealistic. Imagine any fish giving into that temptation! And yet they do, again and again, paying the ultimate consequence.

Temptations that consistently distract us from the most meaningful things in our lives can drain the spiritual energy out of us. One pastor told how it seemed that every time he was going to set aside time to pray or to just be with his family, the telephone would insistently ring with a needy parishioner on the other end. The tempter understands what pulls us away, what lures us and attracts us.

Nonetheless, how do we learn to distinguish between temptations that are truly distractions in our minds and the gentle voice of the Holy Spirit calling us to be cognizant of something that needs our attention? Conscientious people—people who want to do the right thing—especially have difficulty with this.

Steve Lawson describes illicit temptation in this manner:

> The devil is like a dishonest car mechanic. Even if he can't find something that needs fixing, he'll nevertheless tell us something needs to be fixed. In our naïveté, we pay for things in our lives that aren't even broken.[11]

The Holy Spirit draws your attention to things that need a fixing, fixes it and forgets it. That's what forgiveness and maturity in Christian living is about. If you find yourself mulling over past issues, if you feel stuck and spend an inordinate amount of time dealing with "water under the bridge," that's the voice of the tempter.

Desire

I always like to maintain my weight at a certain level. When I go over it by three or four pounds, I diet a little to get back to my desired weight. I had been doing well on a brief diet, and as I headed downtown, I remembered that I'd pass right by a bakery that makes world-class donuts. Driving to my destination, I kept thinking how a glass of milk and a donut would taste so good. As I approached the parking lot near the bakery, my thoughts intensified on this theme.

Then I remembered my diet. So, I prayed a silent prayer. "God, if You want me to stop for a donut, let there be a parking space in front of the bakery." Sure enough, the seventh time around the block... there was the parking space.[12]

I think you will see the source of that temptation. I already wanted a donut and was just rationalizing my behavior. The Book of James puts it this way in an incisive passage:

> Let no one say when he is tempted, "I am tempted of God" for God cannot be tempted with evil and He Himself tempts no one, but each person is tempted when he is lured and enticed by his own desire. Then desire when it is conceived gives birth to sin and sin when it is full-grown brings forth death. Do not be deceived my brethren.[13]

Each person is tempted by his or her own desire. It's not God's fault. We're simply tempted to do what we want to do, anyway. If a person is already leaning in a particular direction, it's much easier to *push* him or her that way.

If you have a bent towards anger, you'll be tempted by situations which are volatile and can push your buttons.

If you have a bent towards lust, your eye will consistently be drawn that way.

If you struggle with covetousness, you'll always want more, even when you obtain what you desire.

Each person is enticed to do the things he or she is already thinking about. You give in long enough to these thoughts and practices, and you develop a habit. Fixate on them, and it can be an addiction.

"Addiction" is an unusual word. Slaves given to Roman soldiers as a reward for performance in battle were known as "addicts." Eventually, the term came to refer to a person who was a slave to anything.

You can become a slave, addicted to nearly anything. Looking at an addict is like watching a wrestling match. (Not phony professional wrestling, but intercollegiate or high-school wrestling.) If a man is flat on the mat as his opponent tries to pin him, the whole home crowd is shouting, "Get up! Get up!" He wants to get up. He wants to break the hold on him, *but he can't*. He desires to be on top, *but he's unable to do it on his own*.

Temptation works a lot like this. You're pulled into an arena of your own choosing, expecting fun, fame and glory, and then you find yourself flat on your back.

Down

Finally, we note that we are tempted when we are down. We get hit hard when and where we are vulnerable. The temptation story of Jesus in the Bible offers us great insight into how this works.[14]

Jesus began His public ministry by being baptized in the Jordan River. The Holy Spirit descended on Him. A voice from heaven affirmed Him. What a great, dramatic start! Then Jesus goes off, full of the Spirit, to fast and pray for forty days in the wilderness to seek God's direction. Who shows up? The tempter.

Can you think of a time in your life when you had a high spiritual experience? You felt whole, confident, full of faith. Then, "POW!" you slip on an old familiar temptation or perhaps a new one, and the feelings of zeal and love just fizzle out of you like a balloon losing air. From the mountaintop to the valley.

There are some obvious areas of temptation catalogued by Christian writers. Some have categorized the main areas as money, sex and power. Clergy speak about being wary of SAM—an acrostic for sex, alcohol and money.

Satan tried to put his finger on the places Jesus would most likely be vulnerable:

Power—"Turn these stones into bread." Satan knew Jesus was hungry, but Jesus replied, "No, it is written man shall not live by bread alone."

Authority—"You can have all the kingdoms of the world if you just worship me." Jesus knew His authority source already, for He countered, "It is written, you shall worship the Lord your God and Him alone shall you serve."

Popularity—"Throw yourself off the pinnacle of temple and the angels will catch you." What a spectacular scene that would be, but Jesus answered, "No, it is written, thou shalt not tempt the Lord thy God."

The Bible says that after failing in this endeavor, Satan left Jesus "until an opportune time." Temptation would return. It always does, especially when we're vulnerable.

Overcoming Temptation

In San Francisco, you can now buy guilt bags—ten for three dollars. If you feel guilty for succumbing to a temptation, just blow your guilt into a bag, pop it and throw it away. That's not so easily done, as most of us expend considerable energy not caving into the temptation in the first place. Here's some help in this serious matter.

First, *remember*. Remember how Jesus acted during His temptations. He quoted Scripture, which gave Him strength to not give in. Three times He said, "It is written...." The psalmist asked:

> How can a young man keep his way pure? By living according to your word. I seek you with all my heart; do not let me stray from your commands. I have hidden your word in my heart that I might not sin against you.[15]

Jesus hid God's Word in His heart. He was the Word of God incarnate. I have memorized many Bible verses that help me when I feel vulnerable. It's in those moments you truly realize the power inherent in the words of the Bible. You remember "that He, Himself has been tempted; He is able to help them that are tempted."[16]

In those fleeting moments when you feel a tug of war within, you can seek a higher supernatural power that will help you be an overcomer.

Even as you remember God's help and model, you can choose to forget past mistakes, sins and times of being your lesser self. One of the beautiful messages of Christianity is being forgiven and developing into a new, vibrant self. Let old things go as you press on to become this new person. It's a choice you must make in your own mind.

The story is told of two monks who were walking in a pouring rain. They came to the edge of a swollen stream, where an attractive young woman tentatively stood, afraid to cross lest she'd be swept up in the current.

One of the monks asked if he could help, and she replied that she needed to cross to the other side of the stream. So, the monk picked her up on his back and carried her across through the swirling water to the other side. Then he and his brother monk went on to their monastery.

That night, his companion said to him, "Friend, I have an issue with you. As monks, we have taken vows not to look upon women, much less touch them. You did both today at the river."

"Brother," the other monk answered, "I put that woman down on the other side of the river. You're still carrying her in your mind."

We also *resist*. When we remember, that's God's part. When we resist, that's our part. It's gathering up strength within ourselves. The Bible says, "Resist the devil and he will flee."[17]

I understand that western sheep ranchers have a novel answer to the problems of coyotes that kill off their flocks. After trying every imaginable electronic gizmo and human ingenuity, ranchers discovered that placing llamas with the sheep thwarts coyotes from attacking.

Llamas don't seem to be afraid of anything. They walk straight toward whatever they see. Coyotes interpret that as aggressive behavior and they won't take on sheep herds where llamas are roaming.

To a degree, we have to be like a llama. Not silly, not underestimating our opponent or spiritual darkness, but in having a fearless approach to temptation. Resist it head on and it flees.

Portia Nelson once cleverly described the learning curve regarding temptation in an autobiography in five short chapters:

Chapter 1—I walk down the street. There is a deep hole in the sidewalk. I fall in. I am lost… I am helpless. It isn't my fault. It takes forever to find a way out.

Chapter 2—I walk down the same street. There is a deep hole in the sidewalk. I pretend I don't see it. I fall in again. I can't believe I am in the same place, but it isn't my fault. It still takes a long time to get out.

Chapter 3—I walk down the same street. There is a deep hole in the sidewalk. I see it is there. I still fall in… It's a habit. My eyes are open. I know where I am. It is my fault. I get out immediately.

Chapter 4—I walk down the same street. There is a deep hole in the sidewalk. I walk around it.

Chapter 5—I walk down another street.

Resistance can mean choosing not to go down the street that leads into temptation.

At the turn of the century, a man was plagued by a problem with alcohol. Just when he thought he was gaining control, he'd fall again, thoroughly humiliated. He was a churchgoing man and he was ashamed of his behavior. Ironically, the saloon was on the same street as his church, just one block down. He finally sought help from his minister. The pastor asked him where he hitched his horse when he came into town. The man replied, "Why, down the street.

There's a hitching post right in front of the tavern." His minister said, "Why don't you change your hitching post, then? Use the post on the other side of the church and you won't have to walk past your place of temptation!"[18]

Jesus told His disciples to pray they wouldn't be tempted. He said, "Watch and pray that you enter not into temptation."[19] Every time you pray the Lord's Prayer, you repeat the words "Lead us not into temptation, but deliver us from evil."[20]

It's resistance knowing that God will back you up, for as Peter says, "The Lord knows how to deliver the godly out of temptation."[20] Don't invite temptation nor miscalculate the power of darkness. We don't want to be guilty of acting foolishly and then asking God to bail us out. I've read that the greatest number of parachutists who die are those who are elite jumpers, those who have jumped at least 200 times. Just because we're strong and mature doesn't mean we couldn't possibly fall hard.

Lastly, *rejoice*. Perhaps that sounds strange to you. Rejoice when tempted? Yet Peter, devoted servant of God, wrote to us "To count it all joy when you meet these trials because they produce patience in you and bring you to godliness."[21]

I think this might be the ultimate picture of a Christian's victory over temptation. He remembered how God is present; he has decided beforehand to resist, and so, when the temptation comes, he can actually laugh it off.

Martin Luther learned the power of rejoicing. He was the key person in the Protestant Reformation. He translated the Bible into the common German language. He was the man through whom the Lutheran Church eventually came about. Luther is one of the great men of history.

But twelve years after the Reformation started, he was severely depressed. Sickness, disappointment and temptation had worn him down. He realized his worst temptations came when he was alone, so he tried to snap himself out of the spiritual doldrums by seeking the company of other Christians and that helped a little. One night he reviewed his recent writings, in which he'd penned three rules for shaking off dull sloth and despondency:

- Faith in Christ
- Get mad
- Win the love of a good woman.

Even this advice to others didn't change him. His only comfort was music, for he wrote, "the devil hates gaiety."

During this time, the temptations and struggles were so deep he wrote, "When I go to bed, the devil is always waiting for me. Life is a constant struggle for faith. Sometimes I meet the devil head on and clash with him."

By late summer of that year, in his agony and despair, he cried out the very words Jesus uttered from the cross—"My God, my God, why hast thou forsaken me?" In that moment, he realized that even in Jesus' moment of despair, the fact He began with the words "My God" was an affirmation of faith.

Luther began saying the words, "My Lord, My God," over and over again. Then, thinking of the thousands of people he'd helped lead to faith in Christ, he began saying, "*Our* God, *Our* God."

Opening his Bible to Psalm 46, he repeated the first verse several times until they sank deep within his soul. "God is our refuge and strength, a very present help in trouble!"

Taking out his quill, Luther sat down and penned these words:

A mighty fortress is our God
A bulwark never failing
Our helper He amid the flood
Of mortal ills prevailing.
For still our ancient foe

Doth seek to work us woe.
His craft and power are great
And armed with cruel hate.
On earth is not his equal.

The writing of these words became transformed into a majestic hymn. It is a hymn that acknowledges the battle goes on, but as Luther eventually was, we, too, can be victorious. And people who experience regular victory usually have a smile on their face and a joy in their hearts. There's even a greater reason to rejoice. You are blessed when you succeed in overcoming. James wrote:

Blessed is the man that endures temptation, for when he is tried, he shall receive the crown of life, which the Lord has promised to them that love Him.[22]

The word "blessing" can be translated as "happy." You feel a sense of rightness and goodness in your life when you live a consistent life.

Let me add one final rationale. Habitually learning to overcome temptation can be a real boost to your self-esteem and spiritual growth. I can recall an incident that was a turning point in my character development.

My wife and I had just enrolled at a seminary where we lived in a large apartment complex for married seminarians. One morning, being the dutiful husband that I was, I took the trash out to the big green dumpster behind our building.

The dumpster was quite full, and even though no one was around, I didn't want to leave my garbage on the ground, which you weren't supposed to do anyway. Instead, through a lot of pushing and shoving, I tried to squeeze my bag into the side door of the dumpster. I succeeded at getting it in, but also caused a shift in the garbage. The contents of another bag fell out—all over my arms and on the pavement.

It wasn't the type of garbage you'd expect to see at a seminary. The bag had been full of cigarette butts and hard-core pornographic magazines. It was so disgusting that it wasn't very tempting. And right on top of all this was a bank receipt for a guy I'll call Mac, who lived two apartments down from us.

I always thought Mac was bit different. He wore his hair very long, had a beard and dressed like an aging hippie. I could handle that with no problem at all, but *this*?

Do I just ignore what I saw? Act like I never saw it?

Should I simply pray he'll get better?

Do I speak to the Dean?

Or should I talk to him?

I was in a real stew for three days. Finally, I was convinced by Scripture in my spirit that it was my obligation to speak to him about his pornography.

Two days later, I saw him at the apartment complex. I summoned up my courage and asked to speak to him for a while. He agreed and we sat down in my apartment. I explained everything that had happened as he rigidly sat the entire time.

When I finished, he paused for a moment (it seemed like an eternity) and offered an explanation. For the past several months, he said he'd been counseling in the inner city with a couple who'd been in bondage over weird and dangerous sexual practices. In the past week they'd come to his apartment, confessed their sin and sought God. As an act of repentance, they'd cleaned all their magazines and paraphernalia out of their van. That's what I had discovered in the seminary dumpster.

I'd never felt more relief in my life. I thanked him for explaining it all to me; we shook hands and he walked out. About a minute later, there was a knock at my door and Mac had returned. He was standing outside, hands on his hips. He said, "Terry, I just want to tell you that was a real gutsy thing to do.

I want you to know I really respect you for speaking to me about this." Then he thanked me and left.

I felt good about myself in that moment. I felt strong, right. My character development took a quantum leap.

I realize now that when you overcome temptation, you gain a sense of wholeness. That wholeness spills into the lives of those around you and comes back reflected to you, strengthening your own resolve to live as the psalmist, who wrote, "Direct my footsteps according to your word; Let not sin rule over me."[23]

The most important thing about you is what comes into your mind when you think about God.

—A.W. TOZER

The danger when men stop believing in God is not that they will believe in nothing, but that they will believe in anything.

—G.K. CHESTERTON

He who leaves God out of his reasoning does not know how to count.

—ITALIAN PROVERB

Wonder is what sets us apart from other life forms. No other species wonders about the meaning of existence or the complexity of the universe or themselves.

—HERBERT W. BOYER

I put the Force in the movie (Star Wars) in order to awaken a certain kind of spirituality in young people—more a belief in God than a belief in any particular religious system. I wanted to make it so that young people would begin to ask questions about the mystery. Not having enough interest in the mysteries of life to ask the question, 'Is there a God or is there not a God?'—this is for me the worst thing that can happen. I think you should have an opinion about that. Or you should be saying, 'I'm looking. I'm very curious about this and am going to continue to look until I can find an answer, and if I can't find an answer then I'll die trying.' I think it's important to have a belief system and to have a faith…"

—FILMMAKER GEORGE LUCAS

Is There Really a God?

I was the kind of kid growing up that was always ready to ask a question or two. I guess I just had an inquisitive mind—or maybe just way too much time on my hands. Consider these questions that still puzzle me:

- Why are there interstate highways in Hawaii?
- Have you ever imagined a world with no hypothetical situations?
- Why do they call it a TV *set* when you only get one?
- Why are they called stands when they're for sitting?
- Why isn't phonetic spelled the way it sounds?
- Why is abbreviation such a long word?
- If a cow laughed, would milk come out her nose?
- What would Geronimo yell if he jumped out of an airplane?

Now, all these questions are humorous, so none of them kept me awake at night. The greater questions, that involve mystery-of-life issues, are often referred to as metaphysical questions or spiritual topics. These are the questions that *should* keep us awake until answered.

Step into any bookstore in America and you will see entire sections devoted to these big questions. That portion of the bookstore may be labeled "Spirituality" or "Religion" or "New Age," but the primary questions about God are present in all. An interesting change in the past decade or so is that Christian titles no longer dominate the religion section. Wiccans, pagans, Buddhism, "New Age" and other practices line the shelves.

Gene Edward Veith eloquently points out this shift:

> As Christianity becomes less of a presence in the culture, ancient pagan religions are rushing into the void. Progressives had always assumed that once Christianity faded, people would do without religion entirely, but that was naïve. Without an advanced religion like Christianity, people are reverting to what came before, to nature worship, neo-animism and primitive superstitions.[1]

As Christianity's influence has been slowly squeezed out of the culture by the courts, an interesting dynamic has occurred. Some academics thought we'd become more advanced as a culture. The reverse is actually true as you see magic crystals, pagan rituals, astrology and gatherings for sun worship, much as humans practiced thousands of years ago.

For those who didn't buy into these "old-new"- age rites, a kind of comfortable god has replaced the God of the Bible. Created in God's image, they decided to return the favor and create God in their own image.

God ends up looking remarkably like the them and their value systems. God becomes this limited, ultra-tolerant, forgiving God who rarely intervenes in the affairs of humankind and doesn't care much about personal morality, except that you treat others kindly (as long as they agree with you!).

Neither of those world views matches up with the faith passed down over the ages. The truth is, all human beings hunger for the supernatural. If you don't have the right supernatural experiences you'll seek out the wrong ones—or try to deny it. The silver lining in all this is that people are asking God-questions, in spite of cultural oppression to keep the issues out of the public arena.

There is a Divine Power and people want to know what God is like and how to relate to God. Over the centuries, thinking persons have come up with various arguments to answer the questions of God's existence. For our purposes, three primary arguments will be very briefly examined: the *cosmological argument*, the *argument from design* and the *moral argument*.

Cosmological Argument

The cosmological argument is sometimes called the *etiological* argument for God's existence. Essentially, it posits that our intricately planned world could not have come into being by chance alone. Someone or something must have caused it to happen.

The logic of this argument is that the cosmos/universe, by itself, is incapable of explaining itself. Since an orderly universe is in effect, it is necessary to assume that a first cause produced it. Think domino effect: the initial cause brought about all resulting effects.

This contradicts perhaps the most popular philosophy taught in American culture today—the philosophy of naturalism. The philosophy of naturalism assumes that nature can explain everything that exists. While taught as if it were a fair-minded science, it is in fact, a subjective, personal world view adhered to much like a religion.

Charles Colson explains:

The real battle is world view against world view, religion against religion. On one side is the naturalistic world view, claiming the universe is the product of blind, purposeless forces. On the other side stands the Christian world view, telling us we were created by a transcendent God who loves us and has a purpose for us. Nature itself is covered with His "fingerprints," marks of purpose in every area of scientific investigation.[2]

C.S. Lewis argued:

Suppose there was no intelligence behind the universe, no creative mind. In that case, nobody designed my brain for the purpose of thinking. It is merely that the atoms inside my skull happened for physical or chemical reasons to arrange themselves in a certain way. This gives me, as a by-product, the sensation I call thought. But if so, how can I trust my own thinking to be true? It's like upsetting a milk jug hoping the splash arranges itself in such away that it will give you a map of London. Unless I believe in God, I can't believe in thought, so I can never use thought to dis-believe God.[3]

The cosmological argument says that naturalists are found severely wanting, often as religious in their fervently held viewpoint as the most narrow fundamentalists. This would lead us to a second argument for God's existence.

Argument from Design

There is some similarity in the argument from design to the cosmological argument. This argument says God's existence is essentially proven through nature. Think intelligent design: there can't be a design without a designer.

It would be silly and absurd to look at a beautifully constructed house, notice how well it was designed and put together, and then assume it all came about by an accident. You'd have to believe there was no architect, no builder for this lovely, intricate dwelling.

Yet that is what naturalists again suggest. We are simply accidents, products haphazardly created over time according to these persons.

Paley's classic watch argument is applicable: Imagine someone finding a watch on the ground while walking through the woods. This person would never conclude that the watch had been lying there forever, a product of soil, wood, minerals and water that somehow came together over the centuries to create this piece of operating machinery.

Rather, noting how the watch parts had been carefully designed to operate in harmonious conjunction with other parts for the purpose of telling time, you wouldn't assume the watch was there by chance. Instead you'd believe an intelligent being had planned, devised and constructed it.

Moral Argument

The moral argument posits that there must be a God (a cause) to account for our sense of right and wrong. Immanuel Kant, the great philosopher, said there were two things that never ceased to amaze him: the starry heavens above (cosmological/design) and the moral law within.

The question has to do with how you got this idea of rightness—or wrongness. How did people all over the world and throughout the centuries gain this sense? Sometimes this is called "natural law," because "by nature" all persons seem to display a sense of rightness/wrongness.

To be sure, a small minority did not have this sense, but they are the exception, like people who are color-blind or tone-deaf. C.S. Lewis believes morality is not just cultural or a personality trait, but a quality of soul. He once used a poignant example regarding helping others. If you see a drowning man, two instincts come into play. One instinct is to save the man and the other is to save yourself. But a third factor soon enters into the picture. It is the higher call that one *must* help the man who is drowning.

This third factor is distinct from the other two. It is an obligation. A sense of compelling ought-ness. It is a moral factor, whereas the first two are instinctual.

Thus, many believe the sense of moral obligation is not just an instinct or something to be taught. Indeed, moral obligation can be taught and become a part of an individual's functioning superego. There are those who suggest that all morality is simply taught—it is education, passed on through relatives and ancestors.

Of course, it is true that much of cultural morality is passed on to us and reinforced through attitudes and behaviors. But where did the concept of right and wrong come about in the first place? Proponents for the moral argument say that source is God.

These three arguments are not listed to be utterly convincing, because the arguments by themselves are not. The truth is, if a person is skeptical and does not want to believe in God, he or she will resist these arguments and come up with alternative and less-compelling rationale.

Codifying Beliefs

Early Jewish and Christian groups codified their beliefs about God. The Old Testament contains an expanding revelation of the nature of God until the New Testament reveals the fullness of God in Jesus Christ.

156

The embryonic Christian church created creeds which were statements of orthodoxy. A creed means to "believe." Creeds are codified belief systems. One of the first creeds of the church came to be known as the "Apostles' Creed." It was not written by any of the original apostles. It was written from the church at Rome.

The Apostles' Creed begins with a remarkable statement about God: "We believe in God, the Father Almighty, Maker of Heaven and Earth…"

The creed begins by saying we believe in God. There is no attempt to prove God in the creed—or in the Bible, for that matter. At the beginning of the Bible, in the Book of Genesis, it simply says "In the beginning, God…"[4] God is just *there*. The writer to the Hebrews says that "Without faith it is impossible to please Him; for he that comes to God must believe that He is—and that He is a rewarder of them that diligently seek Him."[5] Those who truly seek God are rewarded with the comforting and empowering presence of God in their lives.

A World Without Windows

I honestly don't believe there are many true atheists, people who claim to not believe in a God. Most persons who think they are atheists are actually agnostics. Agnostics are fence-straddlers, weighing the evidences. The trouble with most so-called atheists is that they're not examining the evidences. An atheist doesn't find God for the same reason! The Bible says you're rewarded with God's presence if you diligently seek after Him.

A number of years ago, I got involved in an interesting conversation with a taxi driver in Chicago. The cab driver described how he'd had many "religious arguments" with his atheism-professing brother-in-law. His brother-in-law never backed down. Never budged an inch in the discussions. He flatly affirmed there was no God.

One evening, their two families went out together for a meal at a local steak house. During the meal, the brother-in-law suddenly turned pale and began choking and gasping for breath. A large piece of steak had lodged in his throat. A crowd formed around him as the man writhed and twisted on the floor and the only wretched, muffled sounds that could be heard uttered from his throat were, "God... help me...! God... help me."

Miraculously, a rescue team as well as a physician were close at hand. Since the piece of steak was lodged so tightly, they had to surgically remove it to save the man's life. But his true colors were shown in that moment of crisis. His atheism was a bluff, a mask for excusing style and personal practices. He was trying to act like he lived in a closed universe, a world without windows. However, when his life was endangered, his real beliefs were exposed.

So how does one know there is a God? I like the anecdote given by a scholar asked the same question. The scholar used the example of the small boy he'd met who was flying a kite that was so high, it was out of sight. He asked, "Son, how do you know there's any kite at the other end?" The boy's reply: "How do I know there's a kite? I feel the pull of it."

We, too, feel the pull of the Holy Spirit. We feel what Pascal described as the God-shaped vacuum within. That was enough for the ancients and it's enough for the huge majority of people on planet earth. God *is*, and that is where faith is placed.

The Apostles' Creed affirms, "We believe in God, the Father." This is an understanding most succinctly presented by Jesus Christ. Contrary to what some contemporaries have claimed, it is not sexist to call God a Father. If you believe Jesus is the Son of God, revealing God's nature, and knowing that Jesus called God "Father" on many occasions, we refute or slander Jesus Christ by suggesting His language was somehow sexist or limited.

The fact is the Bible uses both father- and mother-imagery.

Both male and female attributes are used to describe God. God is sometimes pictured as a mother cuddling her child, or as a rejected wife or lover.

Jesus entered the mainstream of history not to pronounce that God is male or female, but to say that God cares for you in an especially personal way. Jesus shocked the Jews of His day because He would pray to God in such an intimate manner. He once prayed "Abba, Father." Abba is not just the name of a Swedish singing group from the 1970s. Abba is an Aramaic word meaning *daddy*.

Jesus put a face on God the Spirit; God the supernatural; God the mysterious and replaced these with a loving, compassionate, merciful parent. A Heavenly Father.

The creed moves a step further in our understanding of God. The affirmation states, "We believe in God, the Father Almighty." Almighty means omnipotent, all-powerful.

The people of Israel had a hard time understanding this attribute of God. The Book of Exodus contains a fascinating story of how Israel wrestled with the idea of whether their God was strong enough to protect them in their flight out of Egypt.

God used positive reinforcement to display omnipotence. You may have read how plagues were sent upon the Egyptian captors; how the Red Sea parted so God's people could pass through; how the Israelites drank water gushing out of a rock in the desert; how quail miraculously appeared for food; how edible manna was on the ground daily; a cloud was there to shade them in the daytime and direct them at night. No people in history have ever had such a manifest presence of God.

Negative reinforcement was utilized as well. Those who grumbled were bitten by snakes, swallowed up by the ground, killed by plagues, smitten with leprosy and finally not allowed to enter the Promised Land.

Yet, the stubborn Israelites could not truly comprehend that their God was *the* God. J.B. Phillips once wrote a book, the title of which expresses the problem of Israel: *Your God is Too Small.*

Robert Wells, in his delightful children's book, *Is a Blue Whale The Biggest Thing There Is?* helps us to truly understand what it means to be almighty. Leave it up to a children's book to explain it so adults can understand it:

> The largest animal on earth is the blue whale. Just the flippers in its tail are bigger than most animals on earth.
>
> But a blue whale isn't anywhere near as big as a mountain. If you put one hundred blue whales in a huge jar, you could put millions of whale jars inside a hollowed-out Mount Everest.
>
> But Mount Everest isn't anywhere near as big as earth. If you stacked one hundred Mount Everests on top of one another, it would be just a whisker on the face of the earth.
>
> And the earth isn't anywhere near as big as the sun. You could fit one million earths inside of the sun.
>
> But the sun, which is a medium-sized star, isn't anywhere near as big as a red supergiant star called Antares. Fifty million of our suns could fit inside of Antares.
>
> But Antares isn't anywhere near as big as the Milky Way galaxy. Billions of stars, including supergiants like Antares, as well as countless comets and asteriods, make up the Milky Way galaxy.
>
> But the Milky Way galaxy isn't anywhere near as big as the universe. There are billions of other galaxies in the universe.
>
> And yet, filled with billions of galaxies, the universe is almost totally empty. The distances from one galaxy to another are beyond our imagination.[6]

And the Creator of this universe is God, who with a Word spoke it all into being; who is present everywhere in this universe and beyond and who upholds it all with His mighty power.

God is almighty. As great as we could conceive God's omnipotence, God is even greater than that. In fact, this is the old ontological argument in philosophy. God is even greater than our conception.

We are left, then, with the final statement about God in the Apostles' Creed. "We believe in God the Father Almighty, Maker of Heaven and Earth...." Suffice it to say that the Bible gives no thought to some form of evolutionary development on the part of humankind. While thoughtful Christians may stand on both sides of the issue, the assumption that evolutionary theory has been proven and that any intelligent person must accept it is an enormous falsification of the facts.

Evolution is a theory. A theory with many assumptions not validated by experimental verification. What has occurred at a very small, limited level (micro-evolution) has become an all encompassing theory for life itself (macro-evolution). Even though there is scant evidence for transitional charge in fossil records, paleontologists excuse it as simply record gaps and continue as rigid proponents for their theory—not because of scientific findings, but because of presuppositions about the nature of the universe.

Philip Johnson, law professor at the University of California at Berkeley, has taken these scientists to task when he investigated the claims of Darwinism and its proponents. He writes:

> A point that caught my attention was that the very persons who insist on keeping religion and science separate are eager to use their science as a basis for pronouncements about religion. The literature of Darwin is full of anti-theistic conclusions, such as that the universe was not designed and has no purpose and that we human beings are the

product of blind natural processes that care nothing about us. What is more is that these statements are not presented as personal opinion but as the logical implications of evolutionary science.[7]

Another factor that makes evolutionary science seem a lot like religion is the evident zeal of Darwinists to evangelize the world by insisting that even non-scientists accept that truth of their theory as a matter of moral obligation.[8]

The symposium of the Mathematical Challenge to the Neo-Darwinian Interpretation of Evolution attempted to determine the mathematical probability of evolutionary advance. All the facts, data, assumptions and theories were fed into a super-computer. The computer's final interpretation of the mathematical possibility of evolutionary advance? Less than one chance in ten to the one thousandth power. Take one chance followed by thirty-seven zeroes. Frankly, that takes too much faith for me to believe it. I don't have enough faith to be an atheist. It would fly in the face of all the universe's rationale. In fact, the scientific theory of the origin of the universe—the Big Bang theory—raises interesting issues.

If anything, the Big Bang theory regarding the universe tends to support those who believe in a Creator-God. Cal Thomas notes Philip Johnson, professor of law and renowned apologist. Johnson wrote:

Once theology was the queen of the sciences. Lately it has been replaced by physics, but there are signs that the physicists want to become theologians... Ambitions like this have important consequences.[9]

They certainly do. Naturalistic philosophy regards life as a series of unbroken cause-and-effects that go back endlessly. Charles Colson points out the effect the Big Bang theory has had on this rationale:

But the big bang represents a sudden discontinuity in the chain of cause and effect. It means science can trace events back in time only to a certain point; at the moment of the big bang explosion, science reaches an abrupt break, an absolute barrier.[10]

British physicist Paul Davies, although not a professing Christian, says, "The big bang is the one place in the universe where there is room, even for the most hard nosed materialist, to admit God."[11]

Marvin Olasky has documented the plausibility of the Christian world view in science by collecting analogies that display how it would take more faith to believe in a world without God than to believe in a Creator of the universe. Consider these examples:

- The odds of the Big Bang producing, by accident, an orderly universe as opposed to chaos, are one in one hundred billion to the 123rd power.

- The likelihood of the universe allowing for the existence of life: hitting a target an inch wide on the other side of the observable universe or expecting a pole-vaulter's pole to remain standing, poised on its tip, for centuries following his vault.

- The odds of evolved life? Imagine a blind person solving a Rubik's cube puzzle. Now imagine ten-to-the-fiftieth blind persons (standing shoulder to shoulder, these would more than fill our planetary system), each with a scrambled Rubik's Cube, simultaneously arriving at the solved form.

- Think of a tornado tearing through a junkyard and taking all of the pieces of metal lying there and turning them into a Boeing 747 all at once. This is the likelihood of a created, orderly universe evolving out of nothingness.[12]

Even famous laws of physics lean on the side of the person of faith. The first and second laws of thermodynamics are a case in point. The first law of thermodynamics, which has to do with matter conservation, says that matter cannot just create itself or just appear into existence. It needs something external to bring it about. The Christian faith (along with most religions of the world) say that is God. The second law of thermodynamics is concerned with the law of decay. It states that the universe is gradually winding down into disintegration and decay. So, since it is running down, it must have been once "wound up," so to speak, much like a time-piece. The idea is, again, that the universe had a beginning when it was brought into being.

The conflict for most persons about God as Creator has little to do with the facts and a lot to do with one's presuppositions about life. The apostle Paul knew about this two thousand years ago when he wrote:

> Since what may be known about God is plain to them, because God has shown it to them. For since the creation of the world, God's invisible qualities—His eternal power and divine nature—have been clearly seen, being understood from what has been made, so that men are without excuse."[13]

There is enough knowledge from creation itself to know there is a God. So why is there a problem? Paul goes on to say that the basic reason humans do not know God is not because He cannot be known or understood, but because they chose to rebel against God. "Though they knew God they did not honor Him as God nor give thanks to Him."[14] "They exchanged the truth of God for a lie."[15] "They did not see fit to acknowledge God."[16]

The downward trend of humankind begins with not acknowledging God. The moral issue *always* overshadows the intellectual smoke screen. It is not that men and women cannot believe—it is that they *won't* believe.

Jesus pointed this out to the Pharisees as the very root of the problem. He said, "You *refuse* to come to me that you might have life."[17] Jesus makes it abundantly clear that moral commitment leads to a solution of the intellectual problem. He once said, "If any man's will is to do His will, he shall know whether the teaching is from God or whether I am speaking on my own authority."[18]

Proverbs 18:1 states that he who is estranged from God seeks pretexts or excuses. A student once told a chapel speaker that all his questions about Christianity had now satisfactorily been answered. The speaker asked if the young man had then decided to become a Christian. "No," he replied, "Frankly, it would interfere with the way I'm living."

This honest young man knew the real problem was not intellectual, but moral. We choose to believe or not believe. Everything we believe about God permeates absolutely everything we do in this life. Charles Colson writes that,

> The Christian world view begins with the Creation, with a deliberate act by a personal Being who existed from all eternity... Before bringing the world into existence, the Creator made a choice, a decision; He set out a plan, an intelligent design."[19]

This Christian faith joyfully proclaims there is a God, the Father Almighty, maker of heaven and earth.

My understanding of Christianity is God in search of lost men, not men in search of a lost God.

—RICHARD HALVORSON

What we are is God's gift to us. What we become is our gift to God.

—UNKNOWN

God loves you so much
He loves you just as you are
God loves you too much
To leave you just as you are

—DALE SWAN

A little girl in the second grade had been told to bring her birth certificate on the opening of school. She was found by the teacher, sobbing in her seat. When asked what the trouble was, she said, "I forgot to bring my excuse for being born."

—JOHN C. MIDDLEKAUFF

Cast all your cares on Him for He cares for you!

—1 PETER 5:7

Reach up as far as you can and God will reach down all the way.

—JOHN H. VINCENT

God enters by a private door into every individual.

—RALPH WALDO EMERSON

Is God Interested in Me?

"Looking for love in all the wrong places!"

h, sure, there's a God. Congratulations… that's not too tough to believe, along with ninety-nine percent of the people on this planet. But is God really interested in *you*—your life, work, plans and dreams?

The truth is, most of us are professing theists and yet practicing deists. A theist believes there is a God. A deist believes in God, but not necessarily a transcendent God who takes a regular, active part in the world. Sadly, George Barna reports the most well-known, non-Bible verse (that people think is in Scripture) among Christians is, "God helps those who helps themselves."[1] This is a deistic attitude—very American, very Western in its thought—that suggests we are mostly on our own unless we help ourselves.

While it is true we are to be proactive, involved and productive, we are not alone in this task. The Christian faith proclaims that God is vitally interested in all you are and all you do, and helps you right now, wherever you are. Lest you think I'm talking about pie-in-the-sky theory, let me give you a case in point:

Answers to Prayer

My children both attended a college in northern Indiana. As a lovely Christmas vacation at home in Kentucky drew to an end, they prepared for the 300-mile drive back to school. Eva was registered for a January term class and Asa was joining a college tour group to Greece.

All weekend we followed the weather patterns as the children got ready to head north. Between eighteen and twenty-two inches of snow had fallen in one day at their upper midwest destination. As the storm front and the weekend passed, Monday seemed to be a somewhat better driving day.

Asa had stayed overnight with a friend in Louisville, ninety miles north of us, to get a head start out the next day. He left Louisville at nine a.m. heading for Huntington, Indiana. Remember that nine a.m. leaving time, because it's important to the story.

Eva left in her car from our home in Campbellsville at ten a.m. starting ninety miles south of Louisville and heading to Huntington, the same destination as her brother. Because of the possibly dangerous weather conditions, my wife and I decided to fast and pray for our children's safety all day on the road.

Both of my children later reported to me that about the time they each got outside of Indianapolis, the roads were terrible. They were icy and slick, and blowing snow reduced visibility. Only one lane on each side of the interstate was open for driving, but big transport trucks ventured into the other snow-filled lane and passed traffic, sloshing ice and snow over the windshields of motorists who already could barely see.

Eva reported to me that she would almost frantically run her windshield wiper blades, since her windshield was covered in ice. The ice eventually blocked the wiper solution spigots, so she could no longer clean her windshield and she was forced to drive peering through a small area of the icy windshield.

Finally, yet another huge truck passed her small sporty car and just sprayed it with ice and snow. Eva couldn't see at all, except for one small clearing in her windshield where she saw a green exit sign to her immediate right. She veered her car in the direction of the exit and when she did, the car totally spun around, out of control, down the ice-laden exit ramp.

Fortunately, the car didn't hit anything hard or nailed down, and came to rest beside a snowbank. Eva got out of the car, trembling and tearful, but not hurt. She examined the car and to her relief, it wasn't damaged either. As she stood there, feeling alone and shaken, she looked up... and the very first car coming slowly down the exit ramp was driven by her brother.

Her brother Asa, who had left an hour earlier and ninety miles ahead of her, was making his way down the very same desolate exit ramp. It turned out that he had made several stops to keep his windshield clean, plus had an extended mealtime... and was just pulling off *on that very exit* to get some windshield washer fluid from a service station.

What are the chances that her brother, leaving an hour earlier and ninety miles ahead of her, would pull off at that very exit, at that minute, at his sister's exact moment of greatest need? Coincidence, you say? Circumstances? Not at all. This was neither a coincidence nor circumstantial. It was a God who was more interested in two praying and fasting parents to answer their heartfelt prayers for their children's safety and protection.

Together, they drove their cars to a nearby gas station and each got a gallon of windshield solution. They poured it right on their windshields, drove down the interstate to the next exit, got off and repeated the procedure—and did so all the rest of the way to their college destination.

Jesus Demonstrates God's Care

God is vitally interested in you. This interest is displayed best in the person of Jesus Christ.

Jesus' presence reminds us that God cares. Someone has said that Jesus is the best snapshot God ever took of Himself. Christianity is radically different from most religions in that God comes down and enters into history and time in the form of a human being, Jesus Christ. Most religions have people desperately seeking for God, whereas Christ comes to seek us out. His very mission was to seek and save that which was lost.[2]

Jesus' life displays how God cares for us. Even a cursory reading of the Gospel stories of Jesus highlights a life of constant attention to human need. Jesus was always stopping to talk with people with varying needs, ethnicities and socio-economic backgrounds. There were no barriers. Human beings flocked to hear Him and be touched by Him. Children gathered around Him. Jesus ate meals and conversed with people who were overtly sinning, such as prostitutes and tax collectors. Somehow, while the sin was not condoned, the sinner felt loved, and empowered to change and to be a better person because of the life of Jesus.

Jesus' teaching revealed how God is so interested in all of life. Jesus taught how not a sparrow falls to the ground without God being aware of it.[3] Every hair on your head is numbered, Jesus said.[4] Jesus presented a God who is compassionate, kind, merciful, and just with us. A God who seeks us out.

In the Gospel of Luke, chapter fifteen, Jesus tells three parables of lost things, displaying God's fervent attachment to us. When something of importance to you is lost, it warrants an all-out search. He tells a story of a woman who loses a coin and sweeps the whole house until she finds it. He enumerates a parable about a shepherd who loses one of a hundred sheep and puts all his effort into finding that missing one. Finally, Jesus tells what is now one of the most famous stories in Scripture—of a lost son to a father.

This parable has come to be known as the Prodigal Son story when, in fact, it tells a great deal more about the loving, patient father than the wayward son. This story describes a young man who demands his inheritance early, receives it, then squanders it on reckless living until, destitute, he eventually comes home seeking forgiveness—which he receives abundantly. What insights about God can we gain from this analogy, representing us and our relationship to a Divine Father?

Lessons from a Prodigal

We can note that God loves you so much, *you're allowed to make your own choices.* The son comes and asks for his inheritance early. Under Jewish law, a father was not free to leave his inheritance to whom he wished, as under our laws. He couldn't seek out a financial planner and do with it as he wished with an I.R.A. (Israeli Retirement Account.)

With two sons, the law required him to give two thirds to the oldest and one third to the youngest son. It wasn't all that unusual to divide the estate before the death of the father.

It is interesting to note, though, how money often divides families. This son takes the money and heads south. It reminds me of the guy who won the lottery and phoned home to tell his wife, "Honey, I'm rich. Start packing!" His wife asked, "Well, what do I pack for, a warm climate or a cold climate?" He answered, "I don't care, just be gone when I get home!"

The son had this same attitude. With the money in hand, he felt the tug to leave home… and the father let him go. The prodigal wasn't just leaving home; he was running from the presence of God. Of course, you can't truly do that. You find out, like Jonah, that when you run from God, you end up running *into* God. Nonetheless, you're given the free will to make the choice.

Also note this story is about *rebellion* and *poor choices*. The son quickly runs through his money and ends up taking a job feeding pigs, a task forbidden to Jews. Friendless after the money has run out, he is helped by no one. He is glad to even eat what the pigs are eating.

How has he gotten into such a state? He had his whole inheritance given to him! The story doesn't tell, exactly—just that he spent it on riotous or reckless living. For a very short while, his life was one big Kentucky Derby Party. He spent all he had on things that didn't last very long. Others had been down that road. Surely he knew that. But when you're in a time of rebellion, you try not to think about the consequences of your actions. Keep busy; keep drinking alcohol to dull your senses; keep warding off feelings of guilt and worry.

The prodigal wasted his investment. To be a prodigal, though, you don't have to waste your inheritance. You could fritter away the time God has allotted to you on earth. You could waste a talent given to you. You could waste the resources of your life—your work and income—in a selfish, foolish manner.

The prodigal son really did all these. As he sat there among the pigs, the Bible says, "he came to himself." He had a revelation. He realized what a great father he had and decided to go back home, willing to be a humble servant. D.L. Moody once said that if he could get a person to think just for ten minutes about the state of his soul, he could lead that person to God.

And so, this is a parable with a good ending: the prodigal decides to head back to his father's house. It's a story of *coming home and being welcomed with enthusiasm*.

The son comes home not even daring to ask to be a slave, for they were in some sense a member of the family. The son was going to ask to be a hired servant without any security—who could be dismissed in a day's notice.

The father never gives him a chance to make that request. Dad sees him from far off. He's been looking for his son to return home. When his younger son approaches, he runs out and embraces him.

The father gives him a robe, a sign of honor. Then he gives the son a ring, which is a sign and seal of the authority of his house. Then he gets shoes for his son to distinguish him from a slave, for children of the family were shod in shoes while slaves were not. Finally, a great feast is held.

What an insight into the compassionate heart of God for us! God enthusiastically welcomes us home when we come to our senses. God rushes out to greet us, forgives us and gives us a special place in the forever family.

This is the level of interest Christians believe God has for each one of us. The term "unconditional love" describes the attitude of God. God loves without any conditions. God just loves you, period.

A staff member from the college where I work saw a living demonstration of this at a children's baseball game. After an out-of-town trip, the staff member was just pulling into the edge of our city when he saw a little-league game being played. He hadn't been to a boys' baseball game for many years, so on impulse, he parked his car and went over to watch for a while.

He glanced at the scoreboard and saw it was the last inning with the score tied and two outs. A boy was on third base. He watched as a determined nine-year-old came up to bat. You could see the fire in his eyes. He was going to knock the cover off the ball, bring the man in from third for the winning run and be the hero.

The boy pounded the plate with his bat and tugged at his pants, which were a little too large for him and hung down. The pitcher eyed him and threw the ball. The boy took a mighty swing and totally missed. Strike one.

Not to be phased, the boy still had success written on his face. This was his moment to shine. The pitcher threw a second time, and the boy swung so hard he nearly turned himself around as he missed for strike two.

Now the batter's jaw was clenched. You could see that jaw muscle working as he tightened his grip on the bat and crowded the plate. This time he was going to knock the ball out of sight.

The pitcher reared back, and for the third throw, the boy swung with all that was within him... and missed again. Strike three. He'd failed. Struck out.

Oh—you could see how it hurt. He walked back slowly to the dugout. He tried to keep his head up. He was biting his lip with his teeth to keep it from trembling. A single tear made a solitary path down his chubby cheek. The winning team was whooping and cheering.

It was at this point the staff member became aware of a man to his right, two seats down, sitting in the grandstands. It was the boy's father. And the father, too, had eyes filled with tears. And the father could be heard quietly saying, over and over again to himself, "That's my boy. That's my boy."

Now, do you think the father would have loved his son anymore if the boy had hit a home run? Of course not. And that's exactly how God sees us. Whether we strike out or hit a home run, whether we succeed or fail, doesn't change God's attitude towards us. That's unconditional love. Nothing can change that.

I once read an excerpt from Mary Ann Bird's book, *The Whisper Test*. She came to terms with this truth at an early age:

> I grew up knowing I was different, and I hated it. I was born with a cleft palate and when I started school my classmates made it clear to me how I looked to others. A little girl with a misshapen lip, crooked nose, lopsided teeth and garbled speech.
>
> When schoolmates asked, "What happened to your lip?" I'd tell them I'd fallen and cut it on a piece of glass.

Somehow it seemed more acceptable to have suffered an accident then to be born different. I was convinced that no one outside my family could love me.

There was, however, a teacher in the second grade, whom we all adored—Mrs. Leonard by name. She was short, round, happy—a sparkling lady.

Annually we had a hearing test… Mrs. Leonard gave the test to everyone in the class, and finally it was my turn. I knew from past years that as we stood against the door and covered one ear, the teacher sitting at her desk would whisper something, and we would have to repeat it back— things like "The sky is blue," or "Do you have new shoes?" I waited there for those words that God must have put into her mouth, those seven words that changed my life. Mrs. Leonard said, in her whisper, "I wish you were my little girl."

These are the words God says to every single one of us: "I wish you were My son" or "I wish you were My daughter."

Is God interested in you? That's putting it mildly. God is seeking you out, wooing you, desiring of a relationship with you, fashioned before the very beginning of time.

The glory of God is a person fully alive.

—IRENAEUS

Hell would be getting to the end of your life and finding out you've not been a real human being. Heaven is finding out you are.

—RABBI HAROLD KUSHNER

The fear of the Lord adds length to life.

—PROVERBS 10:27, NIV

If a man's Bible is coming apart, it is an indication that he himself is fairly well put together.

—JAMES JENNINGS

The best fruits of religious experiences are the best things that history has to show.

—WILLIAM JAMES

The harder a man tries to be himself without being right with God, the less like himself he becomes and the more like everyone else he is. Man was made to have fellowship with God; a man is never himself until he submits to this divine rule. Not your talent first, or your money, or your time, or your service, but the complete "you" is what God requests and requires—not that He might make you into a slave, but that He might emancipate you.

—RICHARD HALVERSON

For I will restore health unto you and I will heal you of your wounds, says the Lord.

—JEREMIAH 30:17, NIV

What Does it Mean to Be Authentic?

"Fake it 'til you make it?"

There's a story from the land of India about a man who was walking from one village to another. He was enjoying the beauty of mid-morning. The sun was shining through the little jagged openings in the thick jungle forest canvas. There was a lovely coolness in the air.

Suddenly, a huge, man-eating tiger jumped out from behind him. This cat was hungry! The man cried out and frantically began running as fast as he could, with the tiger in close pursuit.

As he ran, he saw a ravine just ahead with vines overhanging it. With a desperate leap, he grasped a vine and swung towards the other side of the gorge... and almost made it, but not quite. His feet and hands missed the other side and he slid to the end of the vine and hung, suspended there.

The man looked down and it was two hundred feet to the rocks below. He looked up to see the tiger salivating at the edge of the ravine. Then he heard some gnawing sounds and noticed that just above him, out of reach, were some rats chewing on the vine. Well, he was in a real pickle!

As he was pondering his fate, he glanced over to the side of the ravine and there, growing out of its side, was the largest, most plump, delicious berry he'd ever seen in his life. And at the very moment the vine snapped and broke, he reached out and placed the berry in his mouth.

This was a man who knew how to live for the moment.

Most of us don't know how to live very well in the moment. We find ourselves subject to drives that consistently divert our attention from the life that is right in front of us. Alfred Adler, the great psychiatrist, once wrote that he thought we were compelled by two opposite drives:

1. The drive to suppress our feelings of inferiority.
2. The drive to feel superiority.

Life is a struggle between these two polarities and is a result of the sin-nature we all possess. Inferior feelings envelop our minds, so we practice behaviors that make us feel competent, on top of things or superior. And it is not so much what happens to us in life that triggers the feelings, it's how we *react* to what happens that makes the difference.

A number of years ago, in Los Angeles, there were two boys who were raised in a lousy, dysfunctional home with an abusive, alcoholic father. When the boys grew to manhood, they went their separate ways with no contact.

A counselor studying the effects of alcoholism knew this family and tracked down each of the brothers years later. One brother was a hopeless alcoholic like his father. The other brother was a teetotaler, a family man and a pillar of his community.

The counselor asked each of them questions about how they became the persons they were: "How did you become an alcoholic?" "Why did you become a teetotaler and a family man?"

Each gave the same identical answer: "What could you expect when you had a father like I did?"

It's not the events; it's your reaction to life's events that is most significant. Hippocrates once said he would rather know what sort of person has a disease rather than what sort of disease a person has.

Inferiority

I was talking to a professional colleague not long ago. This fellow told me that when he was in high school, he was tall and skinny and wore braces and glasses. Still, he was a decent-looking guy under all that.

In his junior year of high school, he finally mustered the courage to ask out a popular girl with whom he had become friends. When he asked her out, she said, "Look, I like you a lot and you're a lot of fun to be around—but I couldn't be seen out on a date with someone like you."

He was so crushed by her callous, immature comment that it was two years before he asked another girl out on a date. He responded with inferiority. I wish he had thought to himself, "Oh well, that's one girl on the planet who's not interested in me. That still leaves three billion to go!" But instead, inferior feelings engulfed him.

We can react so often in this manner that by adulthood, it's become habitual. Chained to old ways of thinking, past experiences, hurts and wounds, we become stuck.

I understand that once a wild elephant is captured, its captors tie the end of a long chain around a back foot. The other end is tied to a huge banyan tree.

The great elephant will pull with all its strength, but it can't budge the banyan tree. Finally, after struggling for weeks, when the elephant lifts its ponderous foot and feels the chain tightening, it drops the foot heavily to the ground, knowing that further struggle is futile. The elephant has now surrendered to the chain.

At this point the trainers know the elephant is really trapped forever, because it's trapped in the mind. Later, when they take the elephant and chain it to a little iron stake by a circus tent, it never tries to pull away, because it associates the chain with the immovable banyan tree.

How we become chained to past feelings of inferiority! Old thoughts, old sins, past actions remain in our mental closets. Our feelings of inferiority can relegate us to lives of mediocrity.

Superiority

Others of us respond with a need for superiority. We compensate for inferior feelings by becoming good at something or relating to a group that causes us to feel superior or competent.

When movie director Steven Spielberg was a boy, he was small, kind of funny-looking, not the best student and always picked last for football or softball games. Self-admittedly, he was a different sort of kid. But he had a creative mother who knew how important it was for her boy to feel mastery over something.

She sensed his artistic bent, so she bought her son a little eight-millimeter movie camera. She would often check him out of school under the guise of some excuse and they'd spend the day together on the beach or in the forest, creating film stories and translating them into little movies. Eventually, this became his life's passion, and in adulthood he has become one of film's most respected and successful directors of all time.

Former senator and presidential candidate Bob Dole grew up in a poor family who, during the Depression, rented out their house and moved into the basement. When he went off to World War II, he was severely wounded in Italy and spent thirty-nine months in bed trying to recuperate in a full body cast. When they took the cast off his body and Bob Dole looked into a mirror the first time, he was appalled and frightened at the person looking back. He couldn't believe it was him—his body was shriveled. His right arm was totally useless. He was unable to dress or feed himself. From that point on, Bob Dole would have trouble looking into mirrors.

But he made a decision within himself to still make something remarkable of his life. He had to relinquish his initial plans to become a physician because of the extent of his own injuries, so instead he became a lawyer. His wife had to sit with him through law school classes, because he was unable to take notes then. He went on to a remarkable career of government service and fame.

Bob Dole's sister commented that even his race for the Presidency was an attempt to show everyone he'd overcome his handicap. A drive for superiority—rather than wallowing in inferiority.

Interiority

I would suggest there may be another word we could add to Adler's list. There's something more than the need for superiority. There's another way to respond to life.

Father John Powell once coined a term he called *interiority*. Interiority is a sense of who you are within—knowledge of yourself and your relationship with God. To be driven by interiority is to be filled with the spirit of God. Many times the Bible speaks of persons being led or driven by the Spirit:

   Jesus was led into the wilderness.

   Paul was led to the Macedonians.

   Jonah was driven to speak to the Ninevites.

Interiority means you know who you are in God and what you're doing on this planet. And as you begin to know the great, accepting, wonderful love of God, you realize you don't feel so inferior anymore. As you begin to understand your place and purpose in the will of God, your need lessens to show everyone how superior and competent you are.

Paradoxically, at the same time, God's spirit really does empower you to become competent and a person of excellence. This is because you're playing your life out to God and not to the crowd. Interiority is peace with one's self and resultant confidence.

What does it mean, though, to have a sense of confidence in one's self? We are such complex, multi-faceted creatures. Rarely do any of us display all that we really are—nor are we necessarily aware of all we are. For our purpose, let me suggest that you have a *false sense of self*, an *ideal self*, a *real self* and a *revealed self*.

False Self

We've actually covered this construct in other parts of the book under different names. Essentially, your false self is who you think you were based on what others told you. It doesn't mean that others always make wrong assessments of you. Indeed, we can and should get feedback from others we trust about our thoughts, actions and life orientation. This is healthy for us.

However, we can create a persona only to match other people's beliefs and assessments, and this is not healthy. Examples would be the guy who acts in "macho" fashion because he thinks that's how guys should behave, or the woman who creates a wardrobe to cover up who she really is. Or it might involve a frustrated artist who is a C.P.A. because that's what his parents expected him to be. Ironically, we become so used to this false self that it's difficult to separate it from who you really might be.

Ideal Self and Real Self

Many psychologists feel that where we get into trouble is the disparity between our real selves and our ideal selves. Our real self is that which we are at this time. Our ideal self is that which we hope to be or perceive ourselves to ideally be. Religious literature says we are both dust and divine.

Once I spoke to a fellow who was interested in becoming a minister. He felt he had to clean up his act before he could go to seminary. While it may be true that lifestyle changes are in order, the point I tried to make was that we don't come to God and say, "Here I am. I'm all together now. I'm cleaned up. I've become this pristine person so I can be used by You."

It doesn't work that way in Christianity. The Bible says our "righteousness is like filthy rags."[1] Instead, we ask God to clean us up and empower us to become our better selves.

Your ideal self is not your real self. I know it and you know it. And yet we spend a tremendous time and energy trying to act like our ideal selves. It is so important in our culture to be cool, on top of it, fashionable, have enough of the comforts of life and be seen as attractive, witty and popular, that we can get caught on a treadmill. I've seen many women still trying to live up to the impossible Barbie-doll standards of hair, anatomy and lack of blemishes.

A person can become worn out trying to keep up with ideal standards. Psychologists use the term "defense mechanisms" to describe how we defend ourselves against the knowledge of who we are. So much energy is put into defending your ideal self and hiding your real self that it can leave a person constantly tired. And many are!

Bruce Larson once commented that all of us in the church have been taught to play with our cards close to the chest. In other words, don't let people in on what you're really like, because they'll use it against you. And it's true. They will, sometimes.

But if you do that, you slowly start to die. As Jesus said, the more you lay down your life, the more you find it.[2] The more vulnerable you become, the safer you are. The more vulnerable you are, the more real you become.

You can't do it alone. Counselors suggest the best means by which a person establishes congruity between his real self and ideal self is through affirmation by others. The company you keep can lead you astray or lead you to wholeness.

Revealed Self

The fruition of maturity is to move towards your revealed self. This is the person you're becoming. It is the great unknown of young adulthood.

William James, considered one of the fathers of American psychology, held to the premise that after age thirty we didn't change. We were set like plaster. Fortunately, James was wrong, for we indeed do change.

When John D Rockefeller became the only billionaire in the world, he was not a nice person. He was difficult to deal with; he couldn't sleep at night and was unloved by others.

When he turned thirty-three, he was hit by a rare disease. His body became shrunken and all his hair fell out. His physicians gave him one year to live. This traumatic crisis got Rockefeller thinking about his impact on earth, and how he'd accumulated and then hoarded his wealth. He changed and became the world's greatest philanthropist, starting foundations and giving away much of his money to churches and needy people.

His health improved as a result of his changed lifestyle and attitude. Rockefeller lived to be ninety-eight years old.

The Bible says "The fear of the Lord adds length to life."[3] People who live their lives for God and others live better.

Full Benefits Package

Research has now demonstrated that faith is good for your life as well as your soul. Psalm 103 refers to the benefits of being a good person of faith and service.

Imagine you had two comparable persons, one a churchgoer, one not. Make them the same age, working for a similar salary, following similar diets. Which one will live longer? Hands down, it's the person who goes to church.

- In twenty-two of twenty-seven studies, the more often a person went to church, the better his or her health.

- Couples who attended church together even at least once a month increase the chances of staying married and report a much higher level of marital satisfaction.

- People who report that religion is important to them are drastically less likely to have abnormal diastolic blood pressure.

- A twenty-eight-year study of 5,000 people demonstrated that by going to church, you cut your risk of dying prematurely by a third.

Science is even attempting to document the impact of prayer. Experiments show prayer positively affecting headaches, anxiety attacks, healing from wounds and heart attacks.

In one of the more famous studies from San Francisco General Hospital, coronary patients who were prayed for had significantly less complications than those who hadn't been prayed for. They also needed a dramatically lessened amount of antibiotics or other medications. And these patients didn't even know devout Christians were praying for them!

Even the lives of clergypersons are a testimony of the benefits of faith-filled existence. A life insurance study showed that ministers live longer than their peers. The average age at death was eighty-three—eleven years later than the average male. All this despite having to go to school a long time, be paid lower salaries and have constant obligations and a job that's never done.

Your revealed self is when you step into your talents, gifts and a meaningful, moral lifestyle that lifts you up by the bootstraps into an extraordinary existence. It is there for you, and it is there for the asking. It's in your hands.

A wise old man, widely revered for his sage advice, once lived on a mountain. Two young boys decided to trick him. One of the boys hid a small bird in his hands, intending to ask the wise man, "Is what I have within my hands alive or dead?"

If the old wise man replied, "Dead," the boy would open his hands and let the bird fly away. If the old man was to reply, "Alive," the boy planned to crush the bird in his hands.

The boys thought, "We've got him now!"

They went up to the holy mountain and approached the wise old man, who was silently meditating. The boy with the bird in his hands demanded, "Wise Old Man, is what I have here alive or dead?"

The old man looked intently at the boy and slowly said, "It's… in… your hands."

It's your choice to move beyond the false selves of the past and step into your revealed self—your best self.

Unless a man undertakes more than he can possibly do, he will never do all he can do.

—HENRY DRUMMOND

You can't stuff a great life into a small dream.

—ANONYMOUS

After the completion of Disney World, some commented, "Isn't it too bad that Walt Disney didn't live to see this?" Mike Vance, Disney's Creative Director, replied, "He did see it. That's why it's here."

—MIKE VANCE

There is nothing like a dream to create the future.

—VICTOR HUGO

Attempt great things for God. Expect great things from God.

—WILLIAM CAREY

Keep away from people who try to belittle your ambitions. Small people always do that, but the really great make you feel that you too can become great.

—MARK TWAIN

We can never become truly spiritual by sitting down and wishing to become so. You must undertake something so great that you cannot accomplish it unaided.

—PHILIP BROOKS

Is it OK for Me
to Dream Big Dreams?

"Angels imprisoned in stone"

W hen Michelangelo would begin to carve a huge and shapeless block of marble, he said his aim was to release the angel imprisoned in the stone. I view human beings as angels imprisoned in stone. Full of thoughts, dreams, aspirations—each of us is a remarkable creation, only stymied by our usually self-imposed limits.

I was thinking about limits lately. It seems as though the police (God bless them) are cracking down on speeders and enforcing the speed limit more closely. I've only had three tickets in my life, though I've been deserving of more. The first ticket I got was on the day I was discharged from the Army. I was driving too fast, away from the post, with honorable discharge papers in hand. Within twenty minutes, I had another paper in hand—a speeding ticket.

A preacher colleague who was stopped by a state trooper protested, "Be kind to me. I'm just a poor preacher." The trooper grinned behind his big sunglasses and replied, "I know—I've heard you preach!"

It did get me thinking about the topic of limits. Here's a few questions for you:

- Can you sing?
- Can you dance?
- Are you able to draw?
- Could you play the drums?

How did you answer? Imagine I asked those same questions to a four-year-old child: Can you sing? "Oh, yes, I can sing!" The child is likely to burst forth into "Old MacDonald had a farm" right there. Can you dance? "Well, of course I can dance! Just watch me. Everybody can dance!" Can you draw? The child will draw a picture right then and there. Could you play the drums? "Can I? Lemme at those drums! I can play drums."

Small children are so optimistic. They see few limits in themselves early on (which, of course, puts parents on constant hypervigilance mode). Then over time, as the child grows up, various comments will be made.

"You can't dance. You've got two left feet."

"Sure you can sing! Sing tenor. Ten or eleven miles out of my hearing range."

"Your drawings look like stick people."

Amazingly, we believe what people tell us. And slowly, ever so slowly, we construct a ceiling over our potential. Then we put in the walls. Soon, we *are* angels imprisoned in stone.

So is it OK to dream big dreams, anyway, especially for the presence of faith? The answer is a resounding and yet qualified "YES." For we must define what big dreams are.

Big doesn't mean you necessarily get to be rich, famous, important and great. Jesus' teaching on Kingdom living turned that concept on its head when he spoke of greatness in being a servant.[1]

Big means you get to impact the lives and the world in a meaningful, lasting way, as we've discussed in other parts of this book.

You have been graced with gifts that are yours to develop.

They are gifts from God. What you do with them is your gift back to God. God does not take back the gift just because you don't use it for His glory. Paul wrote that "God's gift and His call are irrevocable."

What God will do for the person of faith is plant a little glimpse of a vision within you, a seed of what is to come. That vision is, first of all, a very personal vision for the latent gift within you.

Personal Vision

The writer of Proverbs said, "Without a vision, the people perish."[2] A vision gives you something to hope for; something to aspire to. It propels us beyond the circumstances we see around us.

I love to read and collect stories of people who gain a sense of a personal vision early on and don't let anything detour them from their dreams. I read how Dolly Parton attended a banquet the night before graduation from her small high school in east Tennessee. Each member of the tiny graduating class stood up and briefly described plans after graduation.

One boy announced "I'm going to college in the fall."

A girl stood up and said, "I'm getting married this summer and moving to Maryville."

Eighteen-year-old Dolly Parton stood up, five feet, two inches tall, and proclaimed her plan—"I'm going to Nashville and become a star."

The banqueting hall erupted in hooting, derisive laughter. Ha-ha. Little Dolly Parton become a star?

Reflecting on that experience twenty years later, Dolly said she was initially shocked by the scornful response. She realized, though, it put a steely determination within her to trust in God and God-given gifts and succeed. She says it's funny, sometimes, where we get our inspiration.

Jim Carrey was once a struggling comedian whose act consisted of doing impressions. Then, with his father's support and encouragement, he made the decision to stop imitating others, change his act and go into motion pictures.

One night, after moving to Los Angeles, he drove his beat-up old car to a high hill overlooking Hollywood. There, looking out over Tinseltown, nearly penniless and trying to support two aging parents dependent on him, about to change his act, he took out his cashless checkbook in a symbolic gesture. He wrote himself a check for ten million dollars and wrote it for acting services rendered. He signed it himself, dated it seven years in the future and folded the check into his wallet.

In his mind, he imagined and believed himself to be a successful actor within seven years. He repeated it over again until this vision of fully utilizing all gifts was successfully planted in his mind.

You may know the story from there. Bit parts on shows led to a regular small part on a TV show. His first movie starring role was a surprise hit, and over the subsequent years he became a hot commodity as he reached his seven-year goal. Seven years almost to the very month, Jim Carrey signed his first ten-million-dollar contract to star in a movie.

His father died later that winter. At the funeral, Jim Carrey took from his wallet the old, original ten-million-dollar check he'd written to himself. It was now tattered and frayed at the edges. He put the check in his father's coffin and said, "Thanks, Dad, for believing in me."

There's a personal vision for you out there. It's not to be an impressionist, but to have your own act if you'll be obedient to God.

A Spiritual Vision

This brings a second element into the equation. It's easy to talk about actors and singers and famous people, but what about me? The special component is that, for Christians, the vision has a spiritual ingredient.

In the second book of Kings, Elisha and his servant are in a city surrounded by a hostile army. The servant, afraid, asks his master what they should do. Elisha prays to God, asking to open the "eyes of this servant of mine, this young man, so he can truly see."[3]

The Bible says that the "spiritual eyes" of this servant were opened and he saw that all about him, the mountains were full of horses and chariots of fire. The Lord's host was there to protect them and assist them.

The psalmist wrote, "I lift my eyes up unto the hills—where does my help come from? My help comes from the LORD, the maker of heaven and earth."[4] Our vision is a spiritual one, and so it must be initiated by and sustained by the Holy Spirit.

Robert Schuller came out to Southern California with a five-hundred-dollar grant from his small denomination and a vision from God to build a church for God in Southern California that would reach the world. He started meeting in an old drive-in theater, preaching on top of the concession stand while parishioners sat in their cars. From those humble beginnings, it grew into the magnificent Crystal Cathedral and a television audience that weekly made him the most watched minister in the world.

There are countless stories of faith that equal Schuller's, because when it's a spiritual vision from God, God wants to be proven faithful. His reputation is on the line, so to speak, and the unseen resources of heaven are at your disposal. A door opened here; a gentle nudge there; a seeming "circumstance" happens in front of your eyes. It's all part of being involved in the spiritual fulfillment of a vision for the Christian believer.

One aging mother's vision was to see all three of her sons become Christians before she died and departed this earth. Many of you readers can identify with this mother, who prayed for her loved ones all her life. Two of her sons had come to faith, but her youngest son had not.

She was on her deathbed at a Minneapolis hospital, life slowly ebbing out of her body. Her three sons stood in the doorway. She called them over one by one. She held hands with the oldest son as they talked for a while and then said, "Son, I love you. Kiss your mother now. Good night, son."

Her middle son then came and sat on the edge of the bed. They talked and then she said, "Son, you know I love you, too. Kiss your mother. Good night, son."

The youngest then sat next to his dying mother. They talked for a while and she then said, "Son, you know I love you as well. Kiss your mother. Goodbye, son."

He kissed her and started to turn for the door when he paused and asked, "Mom, why did you say *good night* to my brothers and *goodbye* to me?" The mother answered, "Son, I love you. You're my youngest. Your brothers are Christians and I will see them in heaven. But you've never accepted Jesus Christ as your Savior, so I'm saying goodbye because I know I'll never see you again."

The youngest son cried out, "Oh, Mom!" with a wrenching sob and fell on his knees by the hospital bed. With his mother's trembling hand on his shoulder, he accepted Jesus Christ as his Savior and Lord. And she was able then to die in peace, as this spiritual vision for the children she had borne had been fulfilled.

A writer once asked actor Sean Connery why he still continued to act at his age. Connery's reply: "Because I get the opportunity to be somebody better and more interesting than I am."

That's a truism for a lot of people. They aren't as good as they should be. Their lives' purposes and plans aren't all that noble or interesting. Only God, through Jesus Christ, can take a life and complete the equation to really make it work well.

A Corporate Vision

Finally, this is not only personal and spiritual—it is corporate also—you were not put on this earth in isolation. This vision is never just for you. It's to help others as well. If others aren't being helped in some way, you might want to question whether God is really in this.

My calling has always been in a ministry of higher education. I receive great satisfaction and delight in assisting young adults to think differently about themselves and the possibilities available to them. That's the way life is supposed to work. You love and love comes back to you.

I came to my college at a time when it was small, but with a big vision to help students. Add resourceful planning to a vision that truly tries to make the lives of others better, and the end result is a great story. Today we have triple the enrollment we did when I first arrived, with a vibrant attractive campus full of bright undergraduate and graduate students.

The vision to help others is not just something for the young. It should be a lifelong passion, and a new vision just may emerge.

At an age when most men settle down—the half century mark—Sir Christopher Wren was embarking upon a new career. He'd been serving his whole life as a professor of astronomy at Gresham College and Oxford. He'd decided to become an architect at age forty-eight.

In the remaining forty-one years he lived on the earth, Christopher built fifty-three churches and cathedrals, the most well known being the magnificent St. Paul's Cathedral in London. Most still stand today. Sir Christopher Wren learned the secret that when God puts a vision in your heart, it's not limited to any chronological age.

So, you want to dream bigger dreams? Expand your boundaries. It's scary, I know. But take a risk.

There was a driver who made his way nervously along one of the most treacherous Rocky Mountain roads. He was approaching an extremely narrow pass, and there was no guardrail—nothing to keep him from plunging thousands of feet down the deadly side of the mountain. Then he spied a small sign. It said, "Oh yes, you can. Millions have."

So, you can.

It is not our littleness that hinders Christ; it is our bigness. It is not our weakness that hinders Christ; it is our strength. It is not our darkness that hinders Christ: it is our supposed light that holds back His hand.

—CHARLES SPURGEON

It is never a question with any of us of faith or no faith; the question is always in what or whom will we put our faith.

—ANONYMOUS

He is the source of your life in Christ Jesus whom God made our wisdom, our righteousness and sanctification and redemption.

—1 CORINTHIANS 1:30, PARAPHRASED

My most cherished possession I wish I could leave you is my faith in Jesus Christ, for with Him and nothing else you can be happy, but without Him and with all else you'll never be happy.

—PATRICK HENRY

Life has no question that faith can't answer.

—THOMAS JOHNS

Faith begins when you know that God is always with you and within you.
—DENIS WAITLEY

The most important thought I ever had was of my individual responsibility of God.

—DANIEL WEBSTER

What Does God Want From Me?

rust is the basis for any human relationship. It is faith that the other person won't harm you. It is the belief that the other person is in your corner. If you don't trust someone, you don't really have much of a relationship.

Faith and trust are the primary issues for any baby in his or her first year of life. An infant develops indelible impressions regarding whether the world is a welcoming place and whether other humans will be there when needed. The baby is developing what Jay Belsky calls a "secure attachment," out of which inner faith to caregivers and confidence comes about.

If a child's needs are met consistently in the early years, he comes to believe that these needs will be met in the future. If a child is treated well initially in life, she believes that good things will come her way later.

A survey of college-aged young adults asked about the guiding trait of people who had mentored them and shaped their lives. Overwhelmingly, seventy-nine percent said trust was the most important characteristic, and it was generally exemplified in their parents or grandparents.

In an ideal world, that's how it should be. Trust and faith nurtured in an earthly family would naturally blossom into trust and faith in God and the family of God. And why is faith so important, anyway? Faith is what God desires from you—the trust relationship is at the very core of Christianity. In fact, it is so often called the Christian "faith."

Jesus was once asked an important question. His disciples inquired, "What must we do to do the works God requires?" Jesus answered, "The work of God is this: to believe in the one He has sent."[1]

Do you want to have a life that transcends time? A life of confidence, which in Latin means "with faith?" A life's work that will bring meaning and satisfaction? In Christianity, it all starts with faith.

Faith is different from being good. Most religions of the world stress right actions as a means to salvation and the good life. There are derivatives of the Golden Rule in nearly every religion, but everyone falls short of the lofty goal. Paul Little has pointed out,

> Man's problem has never been not knowing what he should do. His problem, rather, has been that he lacks the power to do what he knows he should.[2]

Often, when people—even professing Christians—are asked why they should get into heaven, they reply that it's because they've been good persons. Yet nearly everyone I've ever talked to acknowledges they haven't been good enough.

Jesus once made an insightful comment about the most "right-acting" people of His day. He said, "Unless your righteousness exceeds that of the Scribes and the Pharisees, you will never enter the kingdom of heaven."[3] The crowds were astonished at this statement from Jesus. They felt that surely, if anyone was good and righteous, it was a Pharisee. The name "Pharisee" meant separatist. Pharisees seriously attempted to live separately from that which was not good or not of God's law.

Jesus was saying that the best of man's efforts fall short. We can't become good enough on our own. Faith is necessary, for "without faith it is impossible to please God."[4]

Faith must have an object. Christianity has spawned a culture in which tolerance and inclusiveness are important values. Yet, an element of narrow inclusiveness makes Christianity stand out: faith is to be placed in Jesus Christ. The writer of Acts, referring to Jesus, said, "Salvation is found in no one else for there is no other name under heaven given to men by which we must be saved."[5]

In the Bible, Jesus asks a great question: "Where is your faith?"[6] He inquires, in other words, where are you *placing* your faith? You will place it somewhere. You can place faith wholly in yourself and your own cleverness. You can place your faith in friends, family, the government or your job. Someday though, all these props for faith will come up short.

Howard Ruthledge was an Air Force pilot who was shot down over Vietnam and served seven years in captivity as a prisoner of war. While confined in Heartbreak Hotel, the name the prisoners had given their POW compound, he came face-to-face with faith. He writes:

> During those longer periods of enforced reflection it became so much easier to separate the important from the trivial, the worthwhile from the waste. For example, in the past, I usually worked or played hard on Sundays and had no time for church. For years, Phyllis had encouraged me to join the family at church. She never nagged or scolded—she just kept hoping. But I was too busy, too preoccupied, to spend one or two short hours a week thinking about the really important things.
>
> Now the sights and sounds and smells of death were all around me. My hunger for spiritual food soon outdid

my hunger for a steak. Now I wanted to know about that part of me that will never die. Now I wanted to talk about God and Christ and the church. But in the Heartbreak solitary confinement, there was no pastor, no Sunday-school teacher, no Bible, no hymnbook, no community of believers to guide and sustain me. I had completely neglected the spiritual dimension of my life. It took prison to show me how empty life is without God.[7]

Howard Ruthledge, air force pilot and POW, became a devout follower of Jesus Christ in that prison. Note the emphasis on being a follower of Jesus Himself, not simply His teachings. Little comments again:

In contrast to the great religious leaders of the world, Christ alone claims deity. It doesn't matter what one thinks of Mohammed, Buddha or Confucius as individuals. Their followers emphasize their teachings. Not so with Christ. He made Himself the focal point of His teaching.[8]

Faith must have an object, and in Christianity, it is focused upon Jesus Christ, the Son of God. Some will claim that is too narrow of a doctrine. Indeed, Jesus said, "Narrow is the gate to life and broad is the road to destruction."[9] He claimed, "I am the way, the truth and the life. No man comes to the Father but by me."[10]

There are those who believe in a contrasting broad doctrine we've referred to earlier as universalism. If you have ever heard someone say that all roads lead to God, you've met up with this illogical doctrine. Though most major religions have some commonalties, the truth claims made by these religious systems differ greatly. They can't all be right. Persons who espouse universalism under the basis of tolerance aren't really considering the core beliefs and the implications of the contrasting religions. In fact, to say all roads lead to God is a slap in the face to most religious systems.

Narrowness is not all bad when it's the truth. It is possible to be loving, kind and tolerant, while still maintaining a firm grasp on the truth of Jesus Christ.

Faith is close by. If faith is so important, how do I obtain it? Can I "work it up" within myself or increase it if I have very little?

A man once brought his disturbed, demon-possessed son to Jesus for healing. The father was in great distress, for no one, not even Jesus' disciples, had been able to help the boy. When Jesus told the man that everything was possible for him who believes, the man cried out, "I do believe; help me overcome my unbelief!" Then Jesus healed the boy.[11]

That's a legitimate prayer. When you don't feel you have enough faith to believe in Jesus Christ to work in your life, you can ask God to help provide the faith. And God will answer.

I once heard Rev. Robert Schuller tell a precious story about meeting Coach Bear Bryant on an airplane. Some consider the former Alabama head coach the greatest ever to coach in college football. Coach Bryant was retired, and after introducing themselves, Dr. Schuller said, "It's always nice to meet another good Christian."

Bear Bryant looked down and replied, "Well, I don't know if I'm a good Christian. I've got a drink in my hand and I smoke, too."

Schuller said, "Any other reasons you think you're not a good Christian?" Bryant answered, "Well, I've never really understood anything in the Bible."

Schuller asked if there were any other reasons. Bear Bryant thought and said, "Well, yes, I've never had the feeling. And I understood if you're a good Christian you're supposed to have the feeling and I've never had the feeling."

Schuller then inquired as to what he expected from a religion. Bryant replied, "I'd like to know that when I die I'll go to heaven. I don't know all that's out there and I don't want to be afraid of what I'll run into."

Robert Schuller said that was something he could help him with and he took Bryant's boarding pass. There was a lot of white blank space on the top and he wrote, "He who comes to me I will in no wise cast out."—signed Jesus Christ. Underneath, he wrote, "I accept that offer." Then he drew a long line, gave it back to Coach Bryant and said, "There's your ticket to heaven, Coach. Sign it."

Bear Bryant signed it, saying, "You know, I think Jesus is the only person who can make that kind of promise." Schuller replied, "You got it."

Then, Coach Bear Bryant took that boarding pass, looked at it, and his eyes filled up with tears. He folded it and put it in his big billfold. He and Dr. Schuller held hands and they both prayed together, with tears running down their faces. And all heaven rejoiced in that moment.

With Bryant's permission, Robert Schuller told the story of their encounter as part of his sermon not long after on his Sunday morning television show. All across America, people heard the story of the most famous college coach in the country accepting Jesus Christ. And the next day—the very next day—Bear Bryant died and went on to be with God.

Coach Bryant's faith was always just a prayer away. In his case, the catalyst was a minister who helped fan the flame of faith within him.

You don't require another person to be there at such a moment. Faith can come from another source as well. Dwight L. Moody once wrote:

> I prayed for faith and thought that some day faith would come down and strike me like lightning. But faith did not seem to come. One day I read in the tenth chapter of Romans, "Faith comes by hearing and hearing by the word of God." I had (up to this time) closed my Bible and prayed for faith. I now opened my Bible and began to study and faith has been growing ever since.[12]

The Bible is a source of faith and it is close by. Open it, perhaps to the Gospel of John or Luke or the Book of Romans, and begin reading; faith will rise up and it will begin to make sense. Your faith is already present in seed form, for the Bible says, "The word is near you. It is in your mouth and in your heart."[13]

Faith also means letting go. Paradoxically, faith is not so much something you muster up. Rather, it is surrender of your striving to do things your way or in your time frame. It is a peaceful confidence that God loves you more than any earthly parent could love. God wants wholeness in your life. Think about God's willingness to be good to you. Consider these attributes of God:

> The Lord is gracious and compassionate, slow to anger and rich in love. The Lord is good to all; He has compassion on all He has made.[14]

This is faith in a God who is on your side. You don't have to strive and search anymore. God gives you power for the journey. The Bible says "taste and see the Lord is good."[15] In other words, try it. You'll like it.

"Letting go and letting God" is sometimes referred to as "resting in the Lord." When you are in the presence of someone you trust, you can relax. You can be yourself, your true self, which was created in the image of God.

Hannah Whitall Smith describes this "resting faith" so beautifully when she asks:

> Have you felt the delicious sense of rest upon going to bed at night? How delightful was the sensation of relaxing every muscle and letting your body go in a perfect abandonment of ease and comfort. The strain of the day had ceased, for a few hours at least. You no longer had to hold up an aching head or a weary back.
>
> But suppose you doubted the strength or stamina of

your bed and had dreaded each moment to find it giving way beneath you? Could you have rested then? Would not every muscle have been strained in a fruitless effort to hold yourself up and would not the weariness have been greater than if you had not gone to bed at all?

Let this analogy teach you what it means to rest in the Lord. Let your souls lie down upon the couch of His will. Relax every strain, and lay off every burden. Let yourself go in a perfect abandonment of ease and comfort, sure that, since He holds you up, you are perfectly safe. Your part is simply to rest. His part is to sustain you and He cannot fail.[16]

What a wonderful thought, that faith is letting go and latching on to God's strength! You let go of old hurts and let God heal them. You let go of old sins and allow God to forgive you. For God wants to release you of all the sins of your past. You let go of your contrived philosophy and embrace the wisdom of Jesus Christ.

Finally, *faith requires a decision.* There is an action component. It is sometimes called a "step of faith," as every doubt won't be answered. It can't be understood from a distance. It must be experienced. Otherwise, it'd be like being taught how to swim without ever entering the water. One must take the plunge, make the step of faith.

What is involved? Essentially, it is establishing a relationship with Jesus Christ, the very Son of God. Recall in your mind the great truths about Jesus Christ presented in this book—how He wants to have a relationship with you; how He desires to forgive you; how He wants to launch your life towards deep meaning, peace and satisfaction. How He totally, lovingly accepts you, just as you are, right now. How, at this very moment in time, Jesus Christ looks deep within your soul and longs to restore communication where it was broken by sin, pride or going your own way.

To respond to Jesus Christ, to accept Him as Lord and God, is known as salvation. It is a bedrock assurance that you are God's son or daughter. Salvation is power to become your true, best self. Salvation is guidance and blessing on this earth and heaven thereafter. Salvation does not mean you've reached your destination; it means the end of your wanderings.

The apostle Paul—the greatest missionary in all of Christianity—once penned these words, as he described how to obtain this lasting relationship with God. He wrote:

> That if you confess with your mouth, "Jesus is Lord," and believe in your heart that God raised him from the dead, you will be saved. For it is with your heart that you believe and are justified. And it is with your mouth that you confess and are saved... the same Lord is Lord of all and richly blesses all who call on him for everyone who calls on the name of the Lord shall be saved.[17]

There it is. Nothing is more important to the whole purpose of your life than making this most significant of all decisions. Perhaps you've never made this faith step. Or, perhaps, you once started this direction and veered off the path.

Shove all doubt aside, and in this moment, pray this prayer with all the faith and meaning you can muster. Your life will never ever be the same. Say the words out loud wherever you are:

Dear God,

I now confess with my mouth that Jesus is Lord and I believe in my heart that God raised Him from the dead. Forgive me for my sins. Forgive me for trying to live my life on my own terms and going my own way. I believe the shed blood of Jesus Christ on a cross forgives all sins, even my own wrongdoings.

Fill my life with power, purpose and peace. Come live with me and give me guidance so that my life will count for something significant.

I now thank you for hearing this sincere prayer. Thank you that I am forgiven. Thank you that my life will change for the better and will have great meaning. Thank you that I am saved and forever will be your child.

In Jesus' name,
Amen

_____

(sign your name here)

Dear Reader, go tell someone of your decision and may you have God-speed on the journey of life. Welcome to your destiny!

Study Guide

Chapter 1: What in the World Am I Doing Here?

1) What are the first thoughts that come into your mind regarding the question "What in the world am I doing here?"

2) When and where do you do your best thinking?

3) Create a storyboard with at least ten scenes. Some of it has already been lived. How would you like the rest of the story line to go?

4) At an emotional level, how does it feel to be spared from being a "Holocaust generation" casualty?

5) Can you think of a time in your life when you had a real moment of clarity where you saw things as they really were?

6) When have you been guilty of "destination disease?"

7) Where are you needed right now in your immediate sphere of influence?

Chapter 2: Who Am I?

1) How does the quote "What I am to be, I am now becoming" strike you? What current habits/practices of yours cause you concern?

2) When were there times in your life when you treated yourself with disrespect?

3) Describe the self-image you developed in your early family years. How did your years of primary education impact that self-perception—positively or negatively?

4) Think back to some early difficulties that caused "psychological scars" within you. How did those incidents shape you?

5) In what areas do you still feel a nagging sense of inferiority? Where have you opted for "safer choices" rather than take a risk?

6) What methods or practices of coping have you used to bolster self-esteem?

7) How have you occasionally laid a charge against God by being upset with your natural features?

8) Respond to the Bible thoughts concerning realizing whose you are, realizing where you're going and realizing what's important.

Chapter 3: What Am I looking For?

1) Billy Graham says Americans are the most bored people on earth. Do you agree? Explain.

2) Where does the drive to acquire more come from?

3) What do you think people are looking for?

4) How do individuals gain meaning in their lives?

5) Why can't pleasure ever be an end in itself? Why doesn't it ultimately satisfy?

6) Have you ever sat around and discussed what you would do if given a million dollars (I know you have!)? What would you do with it?

7) What does the Scripture "The fear of the Lord is the beginning of wisdom" mean to you?

8) Solomon's plan to build a temple for God was his foremost desire. What great thing would you like to do for God?

9) What does it mean to say that Christianity is primarily a relationship?

10) What do the actions of your life tell about what you are looking for?

Chapter 4: What's Really Real?

1) As best as you can, describe your hidden self—the part of you just below the surface that others may rarely see.

2) Think of an incident where, when you waited a day or two until the outcome, it wasn't as bad as you thought it would be.

3) In light of the deep truth that God is especially near when things get difficult, how do you interpret the present times?

4) In what ways has Hollywood's version of reality skewed people's perspectives of life? Think of concrete examples.

5) Can you think of any other activities which people can exalt above God, for example, sports or recreation?

6) Describe a time when your view of the world got bigger.

7) Can you relate to the story about spiritual cleansing? Tell about an incident of forgiveness in your life or in the life of someone you know.

8) Reality is that God looks at you with eyes of love and mercy. If you really began to believe this truth, how might it change you?

Chapter 5: Into What Will I Invest My Life?

1) Describe a time when you came close to death. It may be a near miss, an accident or an illness or any incident.

2) Imagine it's your funeral and three persons of your choosing get to talk about your life. What would you like said about you?

3) Name a person you personally know who seemed to live a rich, full life.

4) What are some noble plans you had early in life to help humanity that you've never carried out?

5) Using the Sower and the Seed parable, how would Jesus describe the "Seed of God's word" in you? How is the seed growing in you?

6) Think of times when you acted totally under your strength without God's help or guidance.

7) Detail a time where you did something right or good and you felt God's pleasure or presence.

8) What would you like to do that would make a difference in the world?

Chapter 6: Can I know God's Will?

1) Name a pet peeve.

2) Can you think of other reasons why people don't use turn signals? Connect the reasons with a spiritual analogy.

3) Paul Little wrote about the mistaken belief that doing God's will makes us miserable. Where does that idea come from and why would people believe it?

4) Why is God's will so mysterious?

5) If you had a calling card describing the work you do for God, what would it say on it? What would your title be?

6) Have you had a time in your life when your actions were guided by a verse from the Bible? Describe it.

7) Did you ever feel a gentle impression or a sense that you were being guided to do something? Tell about it.

8) When have you really missed out on a big opportunity?

9) Perhaps you have a lot of dreams. Tell about a dream that seemed to give you guidance.

10) Identify the significant counselors who have mentored or assisted you at important junctures in your life.

11) "You were born for this time." What does that statement mean to you, and what is significant about your gifts and this time in history?

Chapter 7: How Can I Get the Big Decisions Right?

1) How is faith in God really a calculated risk?

2) Describe times you practiced a "settler spirit" instead of a "pioneer spirit."

3) What were some goals you set for yourself and reached early in life?

4) Was there a time in your life where you "broke away from the pack?"

5) How have you changed since high school days? What new choices for yourself have you made since then?

6) A distinction is made in the chapter regarding strategy and tactics. When was a time in your life plan when you made a mistake in tactics? In strategy?

7) Based on the various factors to consider for vocation, are you in, or preparing for, a life's work that suits you well?

8) How do people go about choosing a life partner?

9) How can you know you've found the right person for a marriage partner?

10) Make a list of all the qualities you'd like in your marriage partner.

Chapter 8: Can I Find Satisfaction in This Life?

1) Define satisfaction.

2) Despite having more, Americans are enjoying it less. Why is this so?

3) Which drives should we give into? Obey your thirst or check

your thirst? What are the advantages/disadvantages of each?

4) Give examples of how security has risen to become a foremost concern to Americans.

5) Describe how the lusts of the flesh, lust of the eyes and the pride of life have caused problems for so many.

6) Why does a selfish lifestyle not ultimately satisfy?

7) Conversely, how can service bring happiness and contentment?

8) How does your disposition toward life impact your level of satisfaction?

9) Think of examples where your acting altruistically (reaching out and meeting other's needs) helped meet your own needs.

Chapter 9: Can I Change?

1) Why do we all resist change?

2) List how the world has changed rapidly just in your lifetime.

3) How were you "scripted" as a child?

4) Tell a story about someone you know of who overcame a scripted childhood and went on to be a successful, happy person.

5) How has your psychological "map" changed in adulthood?

6) How has faith in God changed you?

7) Name some negative behaviors you currently practice that you'd like to be rid of by next year.

8) How does one change, anyway?

9) Life is a do-over. What could that great movie line mean to you, personally?

Chapter 10: How Can I Handle Life's Adversities?

1) Brainstorm about some other beliefs within the "assumptive world."

2) What do you most admire about the life of Joseph? What qualities sustained him through adversity?

3) How have defeats for you turned into valuable lessons? Where have stumbling blocks become stepping stones?

4) Has there been a time when God came especially close to you in your suffering?

5) What positive qualities can be potentially developed as a result of adversity?

6) What negative qualities can possibly occur to persons who deal with much adversity?

7) How can such Bible verses as Romans 8:28 and 1 Thessalonians 5:17 radically change one's perspective toward difficult circumstances?

8) What does it mean to you to "let go and let God?"

Chapter 11: Why Be Good?

1) For what reasons do you act in good and moral ways?

2) Why is morality so important to a nation's existence and progress?

3) How have morals changed in your lifetime?

4) What do you think Aleksandr Solzhenitsyn was referring to when he suggested that America was "morally exhausted?"

5) How did we become a "cut-flower civilization?"

6) What do you think—can we be good without God?

7) Give examples of the dominant philosophy of secularism in early twenty-first century America.

8) Discuss "relativism," "rampant subjectivism" and "excessive individualism" in the culture.

9) How did Jesus Christ and the Christian faith change Western civilization?

10) A follow-up question. Imagine that Jesus had never been born. How might Western Civilization be different?

11) Why isn't so-called tolerance today really not tolerance at all according to William Watkins?

12) In what significant ways does Christianity differ from other major world religions?

13) What are some moral boundaries faced by people of the Christian faith?

14) Why do people so strike out against moral boundaries?

Chapter 12: Can I Overcome Temptation?

1) What is so reassuring about persons who keep their word?

2) Name some of the most common temptations outside of the list in the chapter.

3) Describe how you view the tempter, the personal source of evil in the universe.

4) What kinds of distractions pull people away from their faith and doing right things?

5) Why is there such an enormous problem with addictive behaviors in this country?

6) Give an example of a time in your life when circumstances demonstrated that for every high, there must be a low.

7) Can you think of other creative ways to overcome temptation?

8) How does resistance build spiritual strength?

9) Discuss situations where one could practice Mark Twin's maxim that "it's easier to stay out than get out."

Chapter 13: Is There Really a God?

1) What shifts in interest in "spirituality" have you noticed in the culture over the past few years?

2) How is Christianity's influence slowly being squeezed out of the culture?

3) How are we guilty of creating God in our own image? Give examples.

4) Put the cosmological argument, argument from design and the moral argument in your own words.

5) How has the philosophy of naturalism replaced religion in the classroom?

6) Do you see a place for religion in public schools? If so, how?

7) How do people become moral? What kind of training tends to lead to effective moral development and decision making?

8) Describe an atheistic world view.

9) How does the concept of God as father turn some people off today?

10) Tell about your experience in being presented with theories of evolution. Was it presented as fact or theory?

11) What are the personal ramifications of believing in a naturalistic world view? In other words, how does such a belief system impact how people act?

12) Do you believe the moral issue always overshadows the intellectual arguments as proposed in the chapter?

Chapter 14: Is God Interested in Me?

1) How can you be a professing theist, but a practicing deist? Have you ever been guilty of this philosophy?

2) If someone asked you how you know God is interested in you, how would you reply?

3) Tell about a direct answer to prayer in your life.

4) How does the person of Jesus Christ display the love and interest of God?

5) Since you have free will (allowed to make your own choices), describe times when you made an especially good choice. Describe an especially bad choice.

6) Relate your life to that of the prodigal son.

7) Tell how your level of reception and invitation at your home of origin impacts your perception of a "heavenly welcome."

8) How did the stories of the father and his baseball playing son and the whisper test impact you at an emotional level?

9) Have you had difficulty believing God is interested in you?

Chapter 15: What Does it Mean to Be Authentic?

1) Hillary Clinton popularized the phrase "fake it 'til you make it." What do you think that means?

2) Define authenticity. What does it mean to be an authentic person?

3) How can you learn more about yourself from your reactions than from your actions?

4) Give examples of how you grappled with feelings of superiority and inferiority.

5) How does a person gain a sense of what John Powell calls "interiority?"

6) Describe the disparity and tension between the real self and the ideal self.

7) How can a dynamic Christian faith lead to authentic living?

8) Other than benefits of an authentic faith as described in the chapter, what other benefits are there in being a disciple of Christ?

Chapter 16: Is It OK For Me to Dream Big Dreams?

1) Why do we so readily buy into assessments others make of us?

2) Why do Americans have such an obsession with "bigness?"

3) Who assisted you to have a personal vision for your life early on?

4) How does one gain a spiritual vision for his/her life?

5) Did the stories of Dolly Parton, Jim Carrey, and Robert Schuller build faith in your dreams?

6) How does your personal vision impact the significant others in your life?

7) Have you felt like an "angel imprisoned in stone?" If not, tell about someone you know who fits that category.

8) Explain William Carey's statement, "Attempt great things for God; expect great things from God."

Chapter 17: What Does God Want From Me?

1) Daniel Webster said, "The most important thought I ever had was of my individual responsibility to God." When did you become aware of this awesome responsibility?

2) How is trust the basis for any relationship?

3) Why did Jesus say the work of God was to believe on Him? What does that mean?

4) Many people think they can become good enough on their own. What is Christianity's response to this attitude?

5) How is the doctrine of universalism illogical?

6) How can one increase his/her faith?

7) Describe the paradox of faith: one must hold on and let go at the same time. What does that mean to you?

8) Have you made a choice to have a relationship with Jesus Christ? If it has happened to you, describe that moment.

Endnotes

Chapter 1

1 Psalm 8:3–5, NIV.
2 Psalm 139:13–16, NIV.
3 Psalm 119:59, NIV.
4 Psalm 139:36, KJV.

Chapter 2

1 Job 15:31, KJV.
2 Isaiah 51:1, NIV.
3 1 Corinthians 6:20, NKJV.
4 Luke 16:15, NKJV.
5 Isaiah 55:8, NIV.
6 Proverbs 31:30, NIV.

Chapter 3

1 Ecclesiastes 11:9, NIV.
2 John 1:38, paraphrased.

Chapter 4

[1] 2 Corinthians 10:7, KJV.

[2] Cal Thomas, *The Things that Matters Most.* (New York, NY: Harper Collins, 1994), p. 102.

[3] 1 Corinthians 13:12, KJV.

[4] Craig Bryan Larson, *Illustrations for Preaching and Teaching.* (Grand Rapids, MI: Baker Books, 1993), p. 263.

Chapter 5

[1] Psalm 90:12, NIV.

[2] Mitch Alborn, *Tuesdays with Morrie.* (New York, NY: Broadway Books, 2002), p. 9.

[3] John 15:5, NIV.

[4] Matthew 13:1–23, especially v. 22, KJV.

[5] John 14:12, NIV.

[6] Luke 13:6–9, NIV.

Chapter 6

[1] John 3:3, KJV.

[2] Romans 12:1, paraphrased.

[3] Paul Little, *Affirming the Will of God* (Colorado Springs, CO: NAV Press, 1974), p.p. 11–12.

[4] Psalm 84:10, NIV.

[5] Russ Johnston, *How to Know the Will of God* (Colorado Springs, CO: NAV Press, 1980), p.p. 6–7.

[6] Romans 12:2, NIV.

[7] 1 Peter 2:21, NIV.

[8] Romans 11:29, NIV.

[9] Jeremiah 31:21, NIV.

[10] Psalm 119:24, NIV.

[11] 1 Kings 19:12, NIV.

[12] John 10: 3–4, NIV.

[13] Colossians 3:15, paraphrased.

[14] Proverbs 11:14, KJV.

[15] Psalm 119:105, paraphrased.

[16] Esther 4:14, NIV.

Chapter 8

[1] Andrew Curry, "Pursuing Happiness by the Numbers," *US News and World Report,* December 18, 2000, p. 56.

[2] Ronald Rottschafer, *The Search for Satisfaction* (Grand Rapids, MI: Baker Books, 1992), p.16.

[3] Proverbs 27:20, NKJV.

[4] 1 John 2:16, KJV.

[5] 1 John 2:17, KJV.

[6] Isaiah 55:2, KJV.

Chapter 9

[1] Romans 12:2, paraphrased.

[2] Scott Peck, *The Road Less Traveled* (San Francisco: Harper Collins, 1978), p 18.

[3] Philippians 3:14, paraphrased.

[4] Psalm 51:10, KJV.

Chapter 10

[1] Genesis 50:20, paraphrased.

[2] Psalm 4:1, paraphrased.

[3] 1 Kings 4:29, paraphrased.

[4] Psalm 34:18, KJV.

[5] Psalm 4:6, KJV.

[6] 1 Samuel 22:37, KJV.

[7] John 16:33, KJV.

[8] 1 Thessalonians 5:18, NIV.

Chapter 11

[1] D. James Kennedy, *What if Jesus Had Never Been Born?* (Nashville: Thomas Nelson Publishers, 1994), p.p. 228–29.

[2] Francis Schafer, *A Christian Manifesto* (Westchester, Il:Crossway Books, 1981), p.p. 32–33.

[3] Ravi Zacharias, *Deliver us From Evil* (Dallas, TX: Word Publishing, 1996), p.23.

[4] Ibid., p.23.

[5] Ibid., p.25.

[6] Wade Clark Roof, *Spiritual Marketplace: Baby Boomers and the Remaking of American Religion* (Princeton, NJ: Princeton University Press, 2000), p.9.

[7] Craig Brian Larson, ed. *Contemporary Illustrations for Preachers, Teachers and writers* (Grand Rapids, MI: Baker Books, 1997), p. 123.

[8] Leviticus 10:10, paraphrased.

[9] William Watkins, *The New Absolutes* (Minneapolis, MN: Bethany House Publishers, 1996), p.19.

[10] Ibid., p.23.

[11] Ibid., p. 27.

[12] Galatians 2:28.

[13] Kennedy, *What if Jesus Had Never Been Born?*, p.1.

[14] Charles Colson, *How Now Shall We Live?* (Wheaton, IL: Tyndale House Publishers, 1999), p.23.

[15] Ibid., p.24.

16 Merriam-Webster Dictionary (New York, NY: Simon and Schuster, 1974), p 717.

17 Josh McDowell and Bon Hostetler, *The New Tolerance* (Wheaton, IL: Tyndale House Publishers, 1998), p. 20.

18 Watkins, *The New Absolutes*, p. 37.

19 Ibid., p. 37.

20 Charles Colson, "The Ugly Side of Tolerance," *Christianity Today*, March 6, 2000, p. 136.

21 John 14:6, KJV.

22 I John 5:12, KJV.

23 Acts 4:13, KJV.

24 Matthew 7:12–13, KJV.

25 Paul Little, *Know Why You Believe* (Downer's Grove, IL: Intervarsity Press, 1974), p.97.

26 Psalm 119:45, paraphrased.

27 Genesis 2:17, paraphrased.

Chapter 12

1 Matthew 5:37, NIV.

2 Daniel 1:8, NIV.

3 1 Peter 5:8, paraphrased.

4 Ephesians 6:16, NIV.

5 John 16:33, NKJV.

6 Zacharias, *Deliver us From Evil*, p. 125.

7 Genesis 3:1, paraphrased.

8 Matthew 4:3, NKJV.

9 Nicky Gumbel, *Questions of Life* (London, England: Alpha Books, 1993) p.p. 169–70.

10 Psalm 119:37, NKJV.

[11] Steven J. Lawson, *When all Hell Breaks Loose* (Colorado Springs, CO: NAV Press, 1993), p. 159.

[12] Terry Swan, *Everlasting Laughter*, (Kearney, NE: Proverb Press, 2001), p. 176.

[13] James 1:13–16, NKJV.

[14] Luke 3:4, KJV.

[15] Psalm 119:9–11, NKJV.

[16] Hebrews 2:18, paraphrased.

[17] James 4:7, paraphrased.

[18] Larson, *Illustrations for Preachers, Teachers and Writers*, p. 258.

[19] Matthew 26:41, paraphrased.

[20] Matthew 6:13, paraphrased.

[21] 2 Peter 2:9, paraphrased.

[22] James 1:12, paraphrased.

[23] Psalm 119:133, NKJV.

Chapter 13

[1] Gene Edward Veith, "A God in Their Own Image," *World*. May 6, 2000, p.16.

[2] Colson, How Now Shall We Live?, p. 55.

[3] C.S. Lewis, *The Case for Christianity* (New York, NY: MacMillian Company, 1944), p. 32.

[4] Genesis 1:1, KJV.

[5] Hebrews 11:6, paraphrased.

[6] Robert Wells, *Is a Whale the Biggest Thing there is?* (New York, NY: Albery Whitman and Company, 1993), p.1.

[7] Philip Johnson, Darwin on Trial (Downer's Grove, ILP Intervarsity Press, 1993), p.8.

[8] Ibid., p.9.

[9] Thomas, *The Things That Matters Most*, p. 103.

[10] Colson, *How Now Shall We Live?,* p. 59.

[11] Ibid., p. 59.

[12] Marvin Olasky, "Things Unseen," *World,* April 14, 2001, p. 50.

[13] Romans 1:19–20, paraphrased.

[14] Romans 1:21, paraphrased.

[15] Romans 1:25, KJV.

[16] Romans 1:28, paraphrased.

[17] John 5:40, paraphrased.

[18] John 7:17, NKJV.

[19] Colson, *How Now Shall We Live?,* p.55.

Chapter 14

[1] Barna Research Group, Church Seminar Notes, April 1, 2001, Dallas, TX.

[2] Luke 19:10, NKJV.

[3] Matthew 10:29, NKJV.

[4] Matthew 10:30, NKJV.

Chapter 15

[1] Isaiah 64:6, KJV.

[2] Mark 8:35, paraphrased.

[3] Proverbs 10:27, NIV.

Chapter 16

[1] Mark 10:42–44, NKJV.

[2] Proverbs 29:18, NKJV.

[3] 2 Kings 6:17, paraphrased.

[4] Psalm 121:1–2, paraphrased.

Chapter 17

[1] John 6:28–29, paraphrased.

[2] Little, *Know Why You Believe*, p. 93.

[3] Matthew 5:20, KJV.

[4] Hebrews 11:6, KJV.

[5] Acts 4:12, paraphrased.

[6] Luke 8:25, paraphrased.

[7] Howard Rutledge, *In the Presence of Mine Enemies* (Old Tappan, NJ: Fleming Revell, 1973), p. 34.

[8] Little, Know Why You Believe, p. 97.

[9] Matthew 7:13–14, paraphrased.

[10] John 14:6, KJV.

[11] Mark 9:14–29, paraphrased.

[12] Sherwood Elliot Wirt, ed. *Living Quotations for Christians* (New Yourk, NY: Harper and Row, 1974), p. 76.

[13] Romans 10:8 and Deuteronomy 30:14, paraphrased.

[14] Psalm 145:8–9, paraphrased.

[15] Psalm 34:8, KJV.

[16] Quoted in *Couples Devotional Bible* (Grand Rapids, MI: Zondervan, 1994), p. 548.

[17] Romans 10:9–10, 12–13, NIV.